The Book of Bitches

The Book of Bitches

How to Identify and Defuse The Bitches in Your Life

Erika Lisa Valdez

ISBN: 0692329013
ISBN 13: 9780692329016

For every bitch I have ever encountered.

Table of Contents

Introduction

It's quite the marvel when people ask me, "If you wrote *The Book of Bitches*, then doesn't that make you a bitch? It must be because you know so much about them." I immediately think that any people asking me that question are, well, bitches! It's as if they're putting me on the spot by playing the devil's advocate. Because rather than caring or being genuinely interested in my answer, they've already developed preconceived and ignorant notions. Most of the time, the bitches just want to flip the switch because *they themselves* are bitchy in nature. They want to set the stage and make a play starring me, as if they were the director. *Well, intermission, Bitch!*

Let us break out of character for a second and talk like real people. The fact of the matter is that I myself am not a bitch, but I know many, many bitches. In fact, I know them very well because I've worked in some of the bitchiest industries out there—modeling, entertainment, and pageantry; therefore, I've bumped into fierce bitches repeatedly. After dealing with *so* many of them over time, I began to notice patterns. I realized that bitches are not only found in those industries but everywhere—from your local bitch bank teller to your so-called friends. Know the girl next door? Try the bitch next door! What I have survived is the Wild Wild West of bitches.

I am the number one bitch expert in the universe. Would you like to know my secret to surviving? Identify and defuse a bitch immediately—and manifest your Inner Bitch as well. I'm here to teach you how to master the balance. I don't see a reason to become a bitch yourself unless someone wants to run *you* over. I'm all woman—but I've grown a major pair of crystal/diamond-encrusted balls because that's what it takes to survive in this world of major bitches. I'll teach you how to grow your own set of diamond balls. Enough is enough with bitches!

My go-to secret defense is that I'm not a doormat. Why? Because I learned how to outsmart bitches, which means I can still be nice and kind yet not let them get in my way. Being a doormat is undesirable, but one can pull the plug on such behavior immediately by following the techniques laid out in this book. *You* can cut the umbilical cord of bitchy behavior. However, it takes time and effort, just like using Rosetta Stone.

By using the resources in this book, you can still be your kind self yet be intolerant of bitchy behavior.

I'm here to tell you how to identify bitches in order to gain personal power, retain it, and use it so that you don't get taken advantage of. This book also gives you leverage with bitches, which, let's face it, you will need as life goes on. You can prevent "bitch collisions" by not only recognizing patterns in how others treat you but also by tailoring your behavior accordingly. The problem is (and this is one of the major things I've learned about bitches), you may find that some people you care about (who are bitches) will drive through your emotional neighborhood and ignore your personal roadblocks. They'll do an endless roundabout in your mind, park their cars in your heart's driveway, or worst of all, run you over. This sucks!

As scary as it may sound to all you nice folks out there, ultimately *you* have to grab the bitch by the horns and clear your territory. In order to break through bitch barriers, *you* need to learn how to use some muscle. This is what *The Book of Bitches* teaches. You don't know how to handle bitches because you haven't parked your car in someone else's emotional driveway because of your own bitch tendencies. Most likely, when it comes to the bitches that you deal with, you couldn't park in their emotional driveways or even take a cruise in their emotional neighborhoods if you wanted to, because their emotional crap is blocking *your* own emotional driveway so you can't get even back out—ha-ha-ha! Sounds funny, right? But it's true.

What do you do to stop this behavior? Well, let's start by you getting pumped up and excited to learn about "bitchiness," which is temporary personality malfunction. The good news is that as far as your friends, significant other, pain-in-the-booty boss, colleagues, and even neighbors are concerned, you *can* identify their destructive patterns and defuse them so you can break free of pain and salvage your relationships. Just as importantly, I'm going to teach you that you don't have to become a bitch to get what you want. With my twenty-plus years of bitch experiences in the modeling, television, and pageant industry, combined with my junior high and high school bitch tales, you will see that there is a light at the end of the tunnel, just when you were certain your eyes would get scratched out before you ever saw that light.

This book *shows you* the light. I'm here to enlighten you from my heart and back you up to the hilt so you *will* win your battle against any bitches you may encounter.

PART I
Manifesting Your
Inner Bitch

Hello, my Inner Bitch. It's nice to finally meet you!

Take a moment to envision a burning candle in your heart. This image represents your Inner Bitch. The Inner Bitch glows at a steady pace throughout the day and night when everything is going smoothly in life. Your Inner Bitch is always burning, and keeping it on an even keel is ideal. But when the bitches in your life start testing your patience, that candle flame begins to flicker, and flicker, and flicker. Finally, when a bitch pushes you over your emotional edge, the Inner Bitch flame bursts into an all-out raging porch fire. Grab more than a few fire extinguishers, honey, because the Inner Bitch is raging at that point!

Let's establish one thing up front: the Inner Bitch comes from a good place—it's essentially your self-defense mechanism. However, if you don't read *The Book of Bitches*, your Inner Bitch can go untamed and you risk turning into a bitch yourself. The problem is that with so many people, their Inner Bitches become suppressed through time and personal upbringing, and they have also been influenced both culturally and socially. The lines of behavior have become blurred—thus knowing how to identify bitches and defuse them while not becoming a bitch yourself is a treacherous endeavor. I'm here to keep it simple and help you conquer this wild epidemic of bitch.

Knowing where to draw the line is difficult. People can bully each other and consider it supposedly normal (as we hear about bullying so often), but if you mention emotional self-defense, you are looked at as if you have lobsters crawling out of your ears. The Inner Bitch is that voice that notifies you when you're being taken advantage of or being hurt emotionally. It is an extremely powerful tool when it comes to identifying and defusing the bitches in your life.

There is great power in your Inner Bitch. Many times when our Inner Bitches speak to us, we hear them but don't really listen. Or if we listen, often we don't act. You can listen to your Inner Bitch all day long. You can have conversations with it while taking a poo, take it out to tea, or stroll on the beach with it. But is this really going to stop real bitches from running roughshod over you? I think not. In fact, I know not. What *is* going to stop bitches from running roughshod over you is allowing your Inner Bitch to act out through your mouth and body. For instance, take action and give clues through body language (such as rolling your eyes, sucking your teeth, and snapping your fingers. Snapping your fingers always gets the point across to someone that you *mean business*). You want that "flame" on the inside to manifest itself on the outside when necessary. This usually results in an altercation or an event that lets your offender know that *you know* what that person's motives are—and that you're having none of it.

When manifesting your Inner Bitch, think carefully about how the bitch you're dealing with makes you feel and what the person's offenses have been. Whenever a bitch is testing your patience, make notes on the severity and frequency of the nasty behavior as well as what you would do to defuse the person if you had the opportunity. Your Inner Bitch needs to ponder whether the bitch needs to be shut down verbally, sabotaged in some (appropriate) way, or exposed to others for vulgar, disgusting, and greasy behavior. Documentation is a great tool when it comes to defusing bitches. Does the situation warrant further action? Or, once things are written down, does the situation not seem like such a big deal after all? Utilizing a "bitch journal" is an excellent way of bringing you into better harmony with yourself and discovering what kind of firepower your Inner Bitch has.

From there, you can devise a sensible plan of defense that isn't as severe as your fantasy of tying up the bitch, placing fresh meat all over the bitch, and then unleashing a wild lion out of a cage in the direction of said bitch. Moreover, you can prevent that bitch's thoughts of doing such things to you. Meow! It's also important to identify which types of bitches you're dealing with. I discuss actual bitch types in part *II*. You will use that information to assist your Inner Bitch in identifying and dealing with the jerks in your life, but you'll need your Inner Bitch to whip out a stop sign while also encouraging the smooth flow of traffic. You must be able to manage bitches in a tactful way. This is critical because it is always best to strive to salvage a relationship, no matter what kind of condition it may be in when you sound your horn.

The great news: honing in on your Inner Bitch not only will help you stand up for yourself, but it can also help you promote yourself in all aspects of life. With every bitch encounter you have that is resolved through Operation Inner Bitch (letting your inner fire and lion roar!), you can bet your britches that the feeling of self-respect you get will elevate you to new heights. When you have a goal, whether personal or professional, taking a no-nonsense attitude is a powerful attribute. Again, you don't have to be a bitch on the outside to get ahead. Just knowing on the inside that you won't take anyone's crap is powerful enough.

Many times, I even let my Inner Bitch handle my issues. I'll bury myself under the covers some mornings and moan and pout. Then my Inner Bitch says, "You don't want to get out of bed? Tough, bitch! Get up!" Or if I find myself in a situation where I'm nervous, my Inner Bitch says, "Buck up, bitch! You can do this!" Take your goal, break it down to formulate an equation for success, and execute. You will always have your Inner Bitch as your backup. If you can't do it, your Inner Bitch can.

Your Inner Bitch can be compared to a cheerleader. If you're like most human beings, your lonely little cheerleader is growing cobwebs. As I mentioned briefly earlier, bullying is the norm nowadays in person and through social media—but whatever happened to cheering others on? *What about cheering yourself on through self-confidence*? Take a stand and you'll be able to deal with bitches effectively! More than likely, your Inner Bitch's megaphone has been muffled by bullshit concepts with which society has stuffed and muted it, such as that bullying and picking on others is acceptable. Shake off those cobwebs from your cheerleading uniforms, people, because with my help, you are *back*! There's great power when your Inner Bitch performs back handsprings and flips for no one else but you. She's ready to "rah-rah" at your command and is *your* best cheerleader. It's time to try out your new megaphone, darn it!

As an example, my Inner Bitch showed itself in a big way when I made the cheerleading squad in high school. The tryout process was rigorous, let me tell you! Making the squad was about *my determination*; it was about *defeating the odds*. Your Inner Bitch possesses great power in defeating the odds, in taking that all-important leap of faith and flying across an invisible gap that supposedly exists. The day I found out I was chosen for the team, I questioned whether the word *impossible* really exists, and I decided that it only exists if you let it. This was because all of the other girls who made the team were bred for that shit, and I had never been a cheerleader in my life!

I want you to understand something very important. My Inner Bitch didn't secure my making the squad, but once I *was* on the squad, it helped me to maneuver and survive the wild ride of severe cattiness I was about to embark on. What was disturbing was that a few of the cheerleaders were such assholes that I quit my senior year. Had I had *The Book of Bitches* in high school, I wouldn't have walked away with my manicured bird finger in the air. I could identify them at the time, but I didn't know how to defuse them properly. Even though I've always been aware of my Inner Bitch, I was so young that I didn't have the massive experience that I have now. However, once that episode was over, I began using my *real* cheerleader to my advantage.

So you ask, "How do I manifest my Inner Bitch?" or "How do I connect with it?" Well, the answer sounds simple, but the execution takes work. I like to define it as a complicated splendor that waits dormant inside of you. It encompasses many elements, but primarily your Inner Bitch should only show its face on the outside after you've covered one **major** element: confidence.

Be confident about who you are

There's a theory that no one ever really achieves self-confidence as he or she defines it. It's a dog-chasing-its-tail game. But in the battle against bitches (and identifying and defusing them), there are some keys that are crucial to your self-confidence. The main keys are not to be confused with arrogance but about power from within: who you are, the contributions you give, and the choices you make. We were all born with willpower—we inherently know right from wrong. We have the power to contribute positively or negatively to the world. We were also born with the power of choice. Some people make choices that are wise and worldly, while others make choices that are hasty and thoughtless. Strive to be wise and worldly so you can defuse those hasty and thoughtless bitches. The handiest key of the keys? Your Inner Bitch. Let's examine further.

Your Inner Bitch is your inner power. It's sorcerer-like and magical and is indeed your magic. I unleashed this at a young age, but everyone has this power. Your Inner Bitch is there—waiting, expecting, and anticipating a wake-up call. When you unleash your Inner Bitch and watch it work, you'll be amazed. The more you see the magic, the more magic you can perform—and with a much higher frequency. Your Inner Bitch is what reminds you of what you can do with yourself and your life, and should anyone threaten it by demeaning you, belittling you, or harming you, then your Inner Bitch is there to protect and keep you at full tilt. When you hone in on your Inner Bitch, which is derived from belief in yourself and an unshakable confidence, it will manifest without your even realizing it. Are you ready to learn how to manifest and release your Inner Bitch? One, two three—let's go!

Clutch components to release your Inner Bitch

When releasing your Inner Bitch, you must remember the following: At all times, remain 51 percent sweetheart and 49 percent bitch. Your mantra: Don't dare let anyone push me.

The Inner Bitch is a *business* bitch who takes care of business. It "handles your scandal," so to speak. It's the side of you that lays down the law, tells people like it is, doesn't back down when being cornered, and is a fabulous negotiator when handling a bitch situation. Let's start with the clutch components. These are paramount tips for releasing you Inner Bitch immediately:

CLUTCH COMPONENT #1: Use Sarcasm to Release Your Inner Bitch

If someone tries to alienate you when you are engaged in conversation, don't let that person do so. Practice your sarcasm and pay attention to others' clever comebacks.

If you're with a crowd of people and aren't exactly hitting things off with a particular person, it's likely that at some point, that person will throw a verbal jab toward you. Usually it will be passive-aggressive in nature, so pay attention. It's a small test not only to see if you catch on but also to how you respond. This probing will frequently come in the form of a sarcastic question; but if you're quick-witted, you'll slam the questioner with a sarcastic answer. Your right-back-in-your-face response is a powerful yet subliminal message that you're confident and don't take anyone's shit. Do it with a smile—make your answer as if to be a joke, but after you say your line and are smirking, turn your nose up in the air for a split second whilst looking at the ceiling sideways. Breathe in deeply and bat your lovely lashes. If you can master this technique, wiggle your head very quickly while you breathe—as almost laughing at your comeback line but also saying subliminally to the bitch, "You're a silly bitch!" Keep this up and the person will either back off or find you intriguing. Either way, you win.

When people are getting to know me, they often comment that I'm quirky. It can be rather annoying because I'm really not—I'm quite sassy, as a matter of fact. We all have little personality quirks, but it doesn't mean we're eccentric. I have been called strange, weird, and dorky at some point in my life (mostly in elementary school and junior high), but I've also been called beautiful, intelligent, and lovely. So which is it? If a bitch is putting you down, put a spin on the insults and turn it on its head. My best defense? I turn the insult into a question, asking, "So, am I a dorky weirdo or a weird dork?" Cue the crickets, please!

Some people may try to alienate you by remarking, "I don't get it" after you tell a joke. Here's a good rebuttal: "You don't? I sent it via FedEx, so if you don't get it by Friday, be sure to let me know." If that doesn't flip the person's bitch switch (which is taking them from a snotty, narcissistic mind-set to complete, utter confusion), you can respond, "That's because you need it notarized." The term *notarized* is a powerful choice of word because it totally throws people for a loop. They're like, "Huh?" There's nothing better than turning the tables and seeing them dumbfounded and bewildered. Mega confusion is the scandal here, but the beauty is that the situation is premeditated on your part. And it works.

CLUTCH COMPONENT #2: Use Subtlety to Release Your Inner Bitch

The key to the Inner Bitch is subtlety. If people are the bitches you have them pegged as, they'll know exactly what your sly remark during the lunch break meant. The beauty about it is that they'll have difficulty creating an altercation because it was so subtle. A subtle remark to the outside world can be very clear to them, yet it would be risky for them to make a scene. That's the goal: subtle jab, understood clearly by the bitch at hand yet hard to prove and explain to the general population.

I'll give you an example. When I was in college, a girl had me pegged all wrong. She saw, she hated, and she talked a lot of junk. I was insulted and irritated, but despite her gossiping and muffled laughs when she was at a nearby lunch table, I remained calm and kept her remarks in my mental Rolodex. Eventually, I struck back with tact, poise, and the perfect subtle jab. When the bitch finally lost about fifteen pounds, I told her, ever so sweetly, "Wow, you look great! Did you lose weight?" Clearly annoyed, she replied yes with a muffled sigh.

I was valid in my actions, because she never had reason to make any judgments about me. In addition, she *had* lost weight, so it's not as if I were saying point-blank, "You're an asshole." It was a double-edged sword, a compliment within an insult—a "pig in a blanket." There wasn't enough evidence that I meant it in a negative way, but I knew—and she damn well knew—how it was meant. I assumed (though I didn't really give two shakes of a rat's ass) that she'd finally gotten a taste of the nastiness she so casually expelled in my direction. Was the remark nice of me? Not really—but I said it in such a "pig in a blanket" way that had she called me on it, people probably would've called her crazy. That was what was so great. Others probably would've said, "Well, you *have* lost weight," which would only have irritated her further. I had to give her a put-down, and I did. (By the way, within the next year, once she chilled out and got to know me, we became friends.) A certain charm and poise accompany the qualities of being subtle, so bear that in mind.

CLUTCH COMPONENT #3: Learn to Say "Screw It!" and Cut Your Inner Bitch Some Slack! Start by saying, "Screw the dishes." Feel the empowerment and let it grow. If you really don't want to do something that makes you feel angst or annoyed, then there's no reason to do it. And if there's no reason to, you'll never have to do it. When it comes to cutting your Inner Bitch some slack, you're simply confronting what you want to do with your time and energy and being comfortable with the decision. It's about coming to terms with your likes and dislikes, knowing what you can take or leave, and deciding how much you can bear at once. It's about compromise, honesty with oneself, and self-discovery. Above all, it's about being content in your skin and giving your Inner Bitch a break when you deserve one.

People buckle under the pressures of others and what society expects of them. What ends up happening is that when one conforms, that person is screaming inside because she's simply not doing what she truly wants to do. That's a sad thing! It happens so often in our daily lives: setting aside dreams because people tell us they are too far-fetched, staying with a person who abuses us in some way, just being "in the grind" in general. Because we're so conditioned and on autopilot, often we don't realize how much we loathe doing something. But deep down, we know we are conforming, and that's no way to live. So give your Inner Bitch a break here and there and break free from the chains of bondage!

Personally, I can't stand going to the post office, pumping gas, or cleaning the oven after I've baked. Am I dirty? No. Messy? No, I just have a lot of clothes and makeup. But for fuck's sake, I live alone, and there are times when I've finished my dinner and don't feel like washing the silly plates right away. There's so much pressure in society as a whole to be a superhero. If you're a guy, you must know car mechanics. If you're a woman, you must automatically know how to whip up a to-die-for tuna salad. It's crap like this that taxes our nerves! Grab your Inner Bitch and give it a shaking. You don't have to be a superhero, but in order to keep your sanity to defuse the bitches outside of your home, you need to chillax and let go at times.

If you don't like to go grocery shopping, then don't! Hire someone else to do it for some extra bucks. I happen to take a guilty pleasure in grocery shopping, but I know people who absolutely hate it. As for cleaning, I don't have a lot of time to do it. Granted, I have done it and I will do it, but I prefer not to due to time constraints. If you have to do something but hate it, then throw on your foxiest clothing (within reason if going out in public) and some groovy tunes—whether the tunes are on your headset or in your car—and handle the mission. If *I'm* cleaning, then I at least wear a cute outfit and *always* rock a cocktail ring. But if something truly bothers you, just don't do it. Don't settle or compromise; it's not worth your irritation. You're draining valuable energy, half on the deed and half on the thought of the deed alone. You'll probably find you're avoiding it anyway.

You owe it to yourself to redirect that energy into something positive. You just have to trust, believe, and enjoy the fact that *you* make the rules in your life! If people have a problem with your not doing it, then just ask them what they hate doing most. Getting an answer may be a challenge at first, but everyone has something he or she loathes. We start settling when we resist change, and we resist change when we are full of fear. So just yell, "I'm not gonna do it!" If it's a job you're sick of but you need the income, start searching for something else *immediately*. Half of the time, it's not the job but the people you work with. Something *will* open up if you don't want to work there any longer. Then when you say your good-byes to that job, you can go home, rejoice, and yell, "Because I didn't wanna do it, bitches!"

CLUTCH COMPONENT #4: Get Strong Physically to Release Your Inner Bitch

You definitely have the brains, so why not the booty to match? *Pow!* Punch the crap out of a boxing bag. Pretend *it's* the bitch that's causing you stress. Tell it how you feel! When you're tired and sweaty, take a shower and then ask yourself (or write it down in your bitch journal) how you feel. Do you feel better? If so, rate that on a scale of one to ten, with ten being the best. Have you moved from inner feelings of violence to a place where you could confront the bitch civilly? If the answer is yes, great! We're getting closer to a showdown. If the answer is no, try this: find the piece of equipment in the boxing section of the gym that looks like a bobbing head and stands upright from a platform with a large spring. I like to whack that thing a few times and give shout-outs to my loved ones—punishing it in their honor.

Any cardio with music that stimulates your Inner Bitch drive is also helpful (such as Britney Spears's "Work Bitch"). If the bitch is a person I'm competing with for something, I imagine that person right next to me on the treadmill and I run faster and harder. With exercise, you're not only stimulating your physical muscles, but you're engaging your brain as well so that the Inner Bitch will be released through your body with endorphins. Just thinking about it makes me want to drop down and do two hundred crunches!

I'm not suggesting you run out and buy exercise equipment that will consume your entire living room, buy the latest book on weight loss, or commit to some crazy diet where you can eat all the cheese you want. Please—no more excuses! By not taking care of ourselves inside and out, we stunt our spiritual growth.

Let me get down to a more precise point: *Looking* good (in your eyes) is *feeling* good. It all stems back to your self-esteem. You might be wondering if I have ever had a "fat day" in my life. The answer is yes. I know what it's like to be fat because I once stuffed my face like Porky Pig when I experienced and survived a horrific heartbreak. I lost myself, but I had to regain control. Get started now. Take control today and feel your Inner Bitch start to tingle!

I realize that it can be easier said than done, so please don't think I'm typing away in some complicated yoga position, downing egg whites and a protein shake. It's human to eat unhealthy things or party like a rock star sometimes. After all, you have to stop and smell the roses here and there.

When you take control, jealous or ignorant bitches may not understand and try to derail you with your fitness goals. But learn something quickly and don't forget: You're the only true being who calls the shots. You're the only one who can truly say that enough is enough.

This is why bitches are so hard to defuse—they have no self-acceptance. Self-acceptance is something that requires a lot of honesty with oneself. You may hate life because you have to pay a crapload of taxes, or you just got dumped by some idiot you can't let go of, or your newborn Chihuahua shits everywhere but you're too lazy to train it. This type of shit in life is a given. But *you, you, you* (isn't *you* a great word?) exude more of an aura than you realize just by being right with yourself.

CLUTCH COMPONENT #5 Meditate to Release Your Inner Bitch

That's right! Go ahead and light a candle, place some sage around you, play soft music that you like, sit Indian-style, and meditate that Inner Bitch right on out of ya! Envision an aura with strong colors around you (such as purple and blue), indicating your ability to show compassion for the bitch that you're up against, or you can focus on a red aura, which serves as a subliminal stop sign to that person. You may also want to imagine a protective white light around you that will serve as a barrier when you encounter the bitch. Listen to the music and focus on those auras, knowing that you possess the strength and energy to deal with this person and put an end to the negative behavior.

CLUTCH COMPONENT #6 Have a Light Salt/ No Butter Popcorn Night to Release Your Inner Bitch

Popcorn. Yep, I said it. Now rent the best bitch film classics—like *Mommie Dearest*, *Nine to Five*, and *She-Devil*—and make it a night of inspiration. And keep *The Book of Bitches* close!

Take note of any bitches that you like—and why. Perhaps the scenarios they are in are similar to yours or perhaps some of the characters you watch will mesmerize you with their bitchiness. Maybe some will inspire your Inner Bitch—more than likely, this will be the case. So enjoy the movies, but before you turn in for the night, look in the mirror and quote your favorite bitch lines from the film. You may need your theatrics later, so enjoy this exercise and behold it frequently. But if you do it too much and get crazy with the popcorn, switch to blueberries. Have fun!

If you want to be successful at identifying and defusing bitches, self-acceptance is a requirement. This isn't to be confused with settling. *Settling* happens when you take your current personal situation and adjust accordingly, as opposed to *admitting* your need for improvement and being strong enough to make a stance. And you definitely don't need to settle for bitchy behavior from others, so here is some more bitch food for thought:

Your Inner Bitch has your back

There are some things to be said about manifesting and strengthening your Inner Bitch. If you're the type that consistently gets used, run over, or taken advantage of, you may find it hard to connect with your Inner Bitch. You owe it to yourself to redirect negative energy into something positive. You just have to trust, believe, and enjoy the fact that *you* make the rules in your life!

Here are some basic principles:

> ***Learn to stand up for yourself.*** Your Inner Bitch is composed of a twinge of naughtiness, a smidgen of scheming, and a streak of plotting. It's like the inner voice that would call people out if you had the cojones ("cojones" means a set of balls), blackmail them, or simply get even. The danger lies in deciding when it's appropriate to act on your Inner Bitch's behalf.

The Inner Bitch should never be restrained, though, when it comes to others who are doing the following:

1) Bullying you or ganging up on you … or your bitches (a term of endearment often used to describe your closest friends—I know, the irony!)
2) Accusing you of something that's bullshit
3) Spreading personality rumors or announcing character flaws
4) Trying unfairly to get you demoted or fired from your job
5) Trying to use you for monetary reasons

Any of the above reasons is a total green light for Operation Inner Bitch. The first thing to know is that there are many, many people out there who live in a "Me, Me, Me" world. They view you merely as a tool or a stepping-stone. Or they may view you as something quite the opposite—a *threat*, like a bump in the road. Bitches by nature are selfish, and every deed, action, or decision is based on what will bring them the most gratification. You may truly love helping old people carry groceries, but the bottom line is that you do it in part to be helpful but also for the good feeling you get. This is okay to admit—it's not as if they'll ever know. Even if they did, their own selfish natures will take over because, after all, you're doing them a favor. It is all right to admit this, and it's okay to be selfish at times. If you can at least accept that, then you're ready for some more Inner Bitch prepping. It's exciting! So let go and enjoy the process!

Declare Yourself Bitch for a Day

You've connected with your Inner Bitch—now what? Declare yourself Bitch for a Day (*or two*) ... and let me say congrats! You now know when to zoom full speed ahead and when to ease off the pedal, and you're ready to start exercising your power. Remember, it's easy to misuse the power because people often get carried away—that's why so many types of bitches exist.

But the Inner Bitch should not be misused, for at that point, you've simply become a true bitch yourself. When your Inner Bitch is found and makes a cameo appearance, you may take some people by surprise. This is totally understandable. Up until this point, you have likely been mum, numb, and seen as dumb, to the amusement of certain people. Understand that this sudden spark of character will catch some off guard. The most important, pertinent piece of advice I can give you is to stick to your guns. Fire away!

The first part of being Bitch for a Day is to simply keep oneself from doing anything that's beyond arm's reach. Sometimes it's okay to act like a bitch if it comes from your Inner Bitch.

What I'm trying to emphasize here, folks, isn't that you need to treat your son, daughter, spouse, or anyone else badly "just because." You just have to remind the person that you are in control of your life and you do whatever you please. Here's an example: If you have a spouse you constantly cater to (which I am all for—I'm as domesticated as a cat), then try a small experiment. Instead of having dinner on the table and all that jazz, just be like, "You know what? I didn't make dinner tonight." Your spouse will naturally ask why not in a childlike tone, but don't even give an explanation.

Explaining opens the subconscious floodgates to being submissive. *Screw it!* No explanation. Think to yourself, *My twelve-karat ring is simply too heavy!* Bask for a moment and imagine that you have that heavy weight on your finger for a reason, and henceforth *you deserve a break*. If your family rebukes you, tell them something like this: "I would move if I could, but my ring's too heavy. It does weigh twelve karats, you know." They'll undoubtedly say, "What are you talking about?" You reply, "Well, you know, if I really had a huge ring like that, maybe it would inspire me to get up and cook you something."

If they persist, ask them to do you a favor and buy you one. Hell, tell them to rent you one. Better yet, go out and steal one (just kidding!). If you don't really have the motivation to make dinner, you shouldn't worry or trouble yourself. Treat yourself!

Once you really get the hang of the Bitch for a Day, you'll be able to treat yourself further and start chopping entire words in half while engaging in conversation. The rationale is that you don't have time, and that certainly includes not saying a full word of English if you don't have to. Don't question it. If your spouse complains, gently remind him or her of the saying "Life's a bitch and then you marry one." If you wanted to speak in full sentences and words, you certainly would. But on a day like this, you're in no mood even to glance at your Rolex, and doing anything farther than an arm's length away is just too strenuous. People will deal with it. If they truly want to know what time it is, they'll find out. And why should it matter to you?

You're the ruler and the Supreme Lady of the house. As such, significant others should be told that if they don't control their demands, you won't hesitate to bend them over and spank the ever-loving bitch out of them. Trust me, they'll be totally intrigued. They may bitch a tad further in an attempt to challenge you. But you have already won. In fact, in your eyes, the game never began. If they tease you or try to tear down your royal day, simply say, "You know, I *would* spank you rotten, but, like many tasks today, my heavy ring simply won't allow it." Marvel in that for a while. Treat yourself. If it gets to the point where they're really asking for it, then go ahead and spank them. After all, you're the Royal Jewels.

If family is relying on you for anything, especially money, you will achieve greater power. When pressed for money, tell them they must cooperate first. Remind them of the Golden Rule and ask them if they know what it is; they will most likely look as if they are discombobulated and reply no. This is because, given your behavior, they won't be sure how the Golden Rule applies to the situation.

Let the question linger. Let the answer swirl around on your palate like a savored sip of champagne on a gorgeous Sunday. Once you have them by the cojones in wonder, simply say, "She with the gold makes the rules." If you don't feel like saying anything more, then treat yourself and don't say anything more. Once you can get the members of your family to accept the idea of "treating" you, the energy in the house will be much more fluid. You must stake your ground. It's your day, and you need their immediate cooperation. Treat yourself! Go to the spa or the nearest Ritz-Carlton for the day. Indulge in a nice piece of salmon with—what else?—strawberries and champagne for dessert!

If your family bugs you, harasses you, or just takes you for granted, simply say, "Look, this is my day. Leave your problems with the court jester." Then check your watch (whether or not you're wearing one), look up with a furrowed brow, and assertively announce, "I really don't have the time!" Then leave. Or don't leave. Tell them, "Join me on my journey and partake of my fancy fare. Come enjoy some strawberries and champagne (or sparkling cider), be merry, and chitchat about the bliss I create in our home." If you tell them this, one of two things will happen: either they'll be cool and play along or you'll have puzzled them so much they won't be able to think straight. They may very well leave you alone in your lair, which is fine. That's all you really wanted in the first place!

When to Release Your Inner Bitch

As a golden rule, you don't want to unleash your Inner Bitch if it isn't necessary. Be discerning about the "when and the why" concerning when it *is* necessary. Although the Inner Bitch comes from a good place, it can be both bad and good. It's good because again it's a defense mechanism and one of the handiest keys you'll ever tap into in your life. It can misbehave, however, by subjecting you to harrowing thoughts of what you can do to get even with someone who has caused you harm in some way. Obviously, you don't want to hurt anyone in return, as violence is never the answer, nor is emotional abuse—and some people simply don't know how to regulate themselves so their Inner Bitches are at risk for going postal. In other words, if you explode and get into a screaming match with someone or become passive-aggressive, neither is conducive to the most positive outcome, which is reconciliation. So in the yin-yang world of Inner Bitch, balance is key. Stand up for yourself but don't go buck wild. Use your power to move throughout the cabin and disembark on a negative situation with a bitch.

I'll give you an example of Inner Bitch gone postal. I have a close friend who was referred to as "Miss Firecracker" at her job in car sales. Her Inner Bitch is very strong and usually makes an appearance when she is mentally pressed. She is also subjected to the jealousy of coworkers, as well as coworkers who try to work in on her deals.

Her Inner Bitch has caused her to be written up by her boss several times. In fact, she was recently fired for her outrageous outbursts. This is not say she was reading their intentions wrong, but there are times and places for everything. Control your desire to speak out harshly if you have work troubles. If you let your Inner Bitch go untamed, that could backfire. Bear in mind that along with your inner strength comes control and *tact*. Your Inner Bitch is special; it will show true colors at times, but it should never blind people with its rainbow-like intensity unless 100 percent warranted.

What about when you want revenge? When it comes to your Inner Bitch, you'll have to do some private plotting if you're planning revenge on another person. There may be some perverse thoughts that suddenly make you shudder and say, "I can't believe I just thought/considered/enjoyed that horrible thought." Shortly thereafter, you may talk yourself out of it. A conversation with yourself may sound something like an angel versus the devil:

"I am not that way; I couldn't."
Yes, you can!
"That's a really fucked-up ploy."
Even better!
"Oh, I wish I could …"
You should! You're getting there!
"I can …"
Good job!
"I will."
Go get 'em, tiger!

Engaging in this Inner Bitch mental bantering is normal to a certain degree, but watch out! Analyze what your mind is proposing and decide the subtlest approach to resolving the issue. It's important to remember that your Inner Bitch will keep things under control and the bitches at bay. If you seek revenge, you could become consumed by your own anger and be taken in a direction that is not conducive to a pleasant environment.

It is most certainly the best revenge to be healthy, move forward with goals, and be firm with the bitch. If things get nasty, take the high road and karma will take care of the rest. For all the angst you may have inside, it's wise to manage your feelings and not blow your lid off like a cheap slow cooker that has been used way too many times.

Inner Bitch gone wrong story: When I was in high school, there was this horrible guy who was pretty close to my sweetheart. He was extremely insecure and desperately wanted to part of the in crowd. His desperation was so bad that I practically barfed all over him.

One day at the lunch table, he said something that really pissed me off (I don't recall what, but at the time, it truly struck a nerve). I tucked the insult away into my mental Rolodex. My best friend—who was a witness—didn't care for him either. But we were patient.

When we felt the right day had arrived, my best friend and I both peed in a large cup at the crack of dawn. She kept the cup at work under her register and let it marinate all day. Then, late that night and cloaked in black, we made a quick drive by his house and found his silly little car parked with the roof open. My best friend pulled up next to his car, and I jumped out. I poured a geyser of piss in his driver's seat. It was *total* scandal, *total* inner bitch, and *totally* warranted (or so I thought at the time). Warranted in the sense that not only was he a bitch to me but also to everyone in general. He never would have guessed we did it—he must have been so confused.

Another instance was when my sister's best friend became so infuriated by a male bitch that she went to a pet store and purchased five hundred crickets. She then snuck into the bitch's house through an open window and poured the little bastards into the bed, the hampers, and any remotely dark corner. The beauty of this story is her cleverness. There was no direct evidence that she was the mastermind. It was also clever of her to choose such an insect. Crickets run, hide, and then sing very loudly in search of a mate. And mate they do! Not just frequently, but they also give birth to large numbers. Just imagine this guy coming home, getting into bed, and being attacked by horny crickets. Everywhere he turned, they were bound to appear. I imagine the story ending with the house being tented. *Wow!* Talk about Inner Bitch!

Don't be embarrassed, ashamed, or paranoid over whatever type of revenge your Inner Bitch seems drawn to. As long as it's justified and you're consistently a good person with a positive attitude, then fine! People get tripped out on the idea that others might know what we're thinking, so we suppress these ideas that are a natural occurrence in our minds. I'm not saying you need to go throw your piss in someone's car, but if the thought crosses your mind, at least admit to yourself that you had the thought and then move on. This isn't the Psychic Bitch Network; no one will know your thoughts.

Another reason some people suppress their Inner Bitches and the actions they daydream about is because they must be done in secrecy. Part of the Inner Bitch's essence is that the plans are concocted only by you. Something about secrecy scares good people. That's because good people are usually honest, and shutting down a bitch often becomes secretive. There is a major difference between lying and being deceitful and just keeping your plan mum and executing it. And a plan doesn't mean you're hurting anyone—it could be innocent revenge such as getting a salary raise or a promotion or hot new boyfriend that you flaunt.

Ultimately, you want to get to the point where you don't have to give even an ounce of energy toward revenge or making a point. The Inner Bitch is the strongest when instead of punishing the bitch at hand, it regenerates the negative energy and comes out of it with an almost empathetic view of the person. Once you can master this, you will be free and unaffected by others and their negativity.

As I close this discussion about appropriateness and tact, always bear in mind that sometimes your bitch will just emerge and set a tone. Don't sweat it. If you're justified and are simply putting your foot down for humanity, then make like a Nike ad and just do it! The *best* and *swiftest* way is to work on the down low. Comments, phrases, and small jabs work best because they are hard to prove.

Once again, as I can't stress it enough: don't talk about your plan to anyone else. No coworkers, no mutual friends, *nobody*. If you really need to tell someone, tell your priest.

Anyone else can blow your cover or feed you mindless chatter. People like this that might make you feel guilty or scare you about your thoughts. You don't need that. They have no true clue as to what you and this person have gone through, so why ask them for advice? Fuck it … It isn't worth it. Unless they actually take part in the deed and would be an accessory, write it in a journal and leave them out of it. Then let go of any guilt feelings because obviously your feelings have made your Inner Bitch want to take some action. Don't fight it—just go with it and keep your mouth shut.

Certainly you can do whatever you want. Further, you can handle a situation any way you want. Just because you'd like to give people a taste of their own medicine doesn't make you a bad person or abnormal in any way. However, thinking of bitch shutdown fantasies and actually engaging in them is counterproductive because revenge never solves the problem. The feeling of revenge may soothe the soul for a period of time, but even the greatest acts of vengeance cannot produce true peace. Certainly you can seek *some* type of justice in a legal sense, and you're more than entitled to stand up for yourself, but to act as irrational as the offending party has is childish and a waste of energy.

More than likely, your plot for revenge isn't a pretty one, so part of the Inner Bitch's duty is to recognize this to gauge just how far you're willing to act on it. Daydream the worst of revenges but stop yourself and consider what's worth a risk and what isn't. You can, however, employ the "shutdown technique," as I have found it to have an enormously high defuse rate.

How to shut down a bitch

When the going gets bitch, the Inner Bitch gets going. When you have been suffering in silence, been annoyed in silence, and someone has gotten you all fired up inside, it's time for a shutdown. What goes up must come down, and that, along with your temper, includes the offending bitch. When it comes to shutting down bitches, you must be mentally prepared and confident that this person's behavior is going to stop—today. Here is some shutdown advice:

Know your "downs"

Sometimes a bitch needs *downtime*, so you may need to wait for your chance to strike. There are also times when a bitch simply needs to be *put down*—gently, as if in a veterinarian's office. Finally, there are times when a bitch needs to be *shut down*. When shutting down bitches, you essentially stop them dead in their tracks. There's some controversy involved, but it's worth it because you're worth it. You should have dignity, but if you don't, then get it (for everything else in life, there's MasterCard). Your Inner Bitch has to have one thing straight, though, before you shut a bitch down.

You have to have concrete evidence to go on. If you have witnesses to back you up before you go apeshit, it'll make the shutdown easier. It's best to get something recorded, written, or documented (even if recollecting as best you can in your bitch journal what the bitch has said or done). You'd better be prepared because this is the level when the heat is turned up and things can escalate significantly. A shutdown can involve strangers, higher-ups, teachers or principals, coaches, bosses, and can even cause parent-against-parent spats.

Once when I was on vacation in the Caribbean, I kept seeing the same bitch at the local hot spot. If (her) looks could kill, I'd be nailed shut in a coffin somewhere and no one would be able to find me. She had daggers for me indeed, with that black bob of hers and green eyes that glowed *like a snake's*. I wasn't afraid to stare back at her after the third night, but she had a posse of fellow coworkers with her who picked up on the vibes. She would kill me, and the rest would do the shoveling and cleanup. That's why it's always good to have a wing bitch or two. "Wing bitches" are friends that support you in such situations. One sharp word from my wing bitches and we would have had a riot in the joint. I was outnumbered and was smart to pass on the shutdown, especially because I wasn't in America.

I've been through it all, and I've had to learn how to handle the type of bitch I was confronted with. The bitch in the Caribbean was a Player Hater, and you will learn more about actual bitch types in the next part of *The Book of Bitches*. In hindsight, when situations did get confrontational, it was definitely worth preserving my dignity. On many occasions, I kept quiet and was cordial. I'm not afraid of confrontation, but I don't fancy it or seek it out.

There have, however, been instances where my Inner Bitch has caused me to snap. She spoke her mind vicariously and aggressively through my body, and though it may have caused quite a stir at times, I still give myself two thumbs up for my behavior.

Usually if someone pushes your Inner Bitch too far, you'll have a difficult time controlling it.

Classic bitch story: Let's take a trip back in time to my cheerleading days and discuss how I conducted a successful bitch shutdown. One of my friends wanted to try out for the team, so I devoted my time both day and night to practicing with her. What was my motivation? I wanted her to be with me on the team, and I wanted gratification that I had helped my girlfriend—my best friend—reach her goal. This was turning a goal into a hard-core achievement!

She became a cheerleader all right, and because she was so petite, in a lot of stunts, she was thrown up in the air as fast as Tinker Bell can cast her wand. An amazing flyer, she struck poses with which even the most experienced girls struggled.

We were just part of a group of sixteen- and seventeen-year-olds, ragingly hormonal and completely caught up in the social echelon that high school presents. Jealousy runs rampant at this age, escalating the number of bitches. But while my best friend was soaring high in a cheerleading stunt, this jealous bitch on our squad was gossiping and giggling about her. This bitch didn't like me anyway, as I knew what kind of person she was. In her eyes, I was partially responsible for bringing "competition" to the scene.

This harassment went on for days, and soon she began to irritate me. There was something more deeply rooted than just what appeared on the surface. Up until the moment I'm about to describe, I had filed her remarks, her facial expressions, and her vibes into my mental Rolodex.

But when she started to concentrate her hate on my best friend, I went berserk. One day at practice, she was completely taken aback when I put my hands on my hips, looked her straight in the eye, and said, "What are *you* laughing at?"

Her expression was like a deer in the headlights. So I asked her again, this time dropping the F-bomb: "What the *fuck* are you laughing at, bitch?" That was appalling and completely unexpected. In slow motion, the other cheerleaders turned their heads toward me and then back to her. Everyone was clearly shocked by the exchange.

This had to be done. Enough was enough, for God's sake. And at the time, since it was high school, it was a big, dramatic ordeal. I remember going home and thinking, *Oh, Valdez, what have you started?* But here we are, over fifteen years later, and the whole incident doesn't matter one bit. Nothing extraordinary happened from the event, and we even made up eventually. But to this day, I'm glad I stood up for my friend that afternoon. A shutdown is a last-resort tactic, but things may come to the point where the shutdown needs to occur. Yes, that day I identified the bitch and defused her *by shutting her ass down*. That's dealing with a bitch all right, and I was never bothered again—and neither was my friend. In general, however, you'll want to know when to keep your temper in check and when it's time for a shutdown. But if it's time, by all means handle it!

Transcending bitches

The ultimate goal of identifying and defusing bitches is to transcend them. When a bitch is transcended from bitchdom, it means she finally got off her bitch horse. It also means that you've successfully pointed out her bitch characteristics and have worked with her to become a quality human being. It's almost as if she had never seen her face and suddenly you held a mirror up to her. She may screech at what she sees, squeal, and try to run, but *not so fast*! You force her to stay and take a close look at herself.

Transcending a bitch means not giving up on someone. It means believing in someone. It means believing that under all that bitchiness is a person capable of being loving, trusting, and not being such a … bitch. By using the tactics described in this book, you will be delighted at how many bitches can be defused and transcended from a level of negative bitch to a level of positively nice.

This is particularly true with bitches you are also friends with, but it can absolutely apply to almost any bitch. When a bitch is transcended, a lightbulb goes off and suddenly she gets it. She gets herself. She gets where you're coming from. At that point in her mind, it's all good.

Transcending a bitch is like her being trapped in a black hole for a lengthy time and then suddenly you yank her out of there and she loves you for it.

You know a bitch is transcended when you actually start to like the person, she starts to like you too, and any bitchy behavior that brought you grief has ceased. It is a joyous feeling because you know that the relationship has been salvaged—not only that: it is positioned to grow.

You want to transcend all bitches, but you must pick your battles. You can't expect yourself to defuse all of them. That's exhausting. My advice to you is to look at the bitches around you, choose the ones (or one) that you see has the most true friendship potential, and go from there. You may not want to bother with anyone currently, but eventually you will—even if it's for the sake of getting along at work. You will wish to develop more with that person. Although you may also want to transcend a bitch for that person's sake, the result will be a flourishing relationship.

This is not to be confused with shutting a bitch down. Transcending is when others realize their faults and behaviors and work with you for a change for the better. Shutting them down is stopping them in their tracks—period.

The only bitch that cannot be transcended is the Player Hater, and that is because that bitch's problems stem from low self-esteem. The Inner Bitch is the antithesis of low self-esteem. Player Haters are so spiteful, envious, and hating that they are capable of wreaking havoc in others' lives. People like that cannot do you any good whatsoever.

Some valid questions are worth asking when deciding whether the bitches in question are worth tolerating: What type of bitch are they? What can you learn from them? Do they know they're being bitches? Can they be *transcended?*

Although we aren't striving for miracles here, nothing is impossible. Still, for a relationship to have a shot, you must remain calm and patient. Until you completely understand people, you won't know if they can be transcended from bitchdom. When I look at the numbers of bitches I've dealt with over the years, only a handful of cases were hopeless. As you will see, these hopeless cases serve as the basis for our first bitch up to bat, the Player Hater.

PART II
The Bitches

The Hierarchy of Bitches

Big Bad Bitches (monsters that breathe fire and are ready to roast ya)

These bitches are the most difficult to deal with. Tough as nails, and sometimes harder to tackle than an all-star quarterback, these individuals are heavily drenched in bitch. They're the most difficult to transcend because their bitchy mind-sets, attitudes, and perceptions are strongly ingrained. They are like stone—and they like to cast stones too. But have no fear! I will lay them out one by one so you can identify them for the bitches they are. Most likely, they've behaved like Big Bad Bitches for a very long time and have gotten away with chewing people up and spitting them out. They're like tornadoes in that the more momentum they pick up, the larger they grow. It's very likely that the Big Bad Bitches you're dealing with relish in the power they feel when they have dominated someone, which only darkens their perception of the big picture. The majority of the time, a Big Bad Bitch requires the shutdown technique on at least one level. This is why it's helpful to write down offenses, dates, general evidence, and witnesses. The Inner Bitch must be very strong in order to show Big Bad Bitches that you can rise to their occasions and extinguish the fire they breathe.

Good Witch Bitches (they have magical wands that they beat you with on occasion)

These are interesting types because for the most part, they're good people, and it's easy to see their positive traits. However, it's fairly easy to see their negative traits as well. These bitches operate like a light switch—off and on, up and down. If the switch gets flipped too many times, the whole damn bulb goes out. It can be a three-ring circus—fire, acrobatics, and lots of juggling, flying around, and balancing. They have the power and magic to wave their lovely "friendship wands" over your head and then *bam*! They crack you over the head with them. They often mean no true harm, but they're so oblivious to their bitchy behavior that it gets to the point where you want to snatch their wands and shove them up their asses. They can pull off some very unconventional bitch behavior, and you will often discover that people you interact with on a consistent basis are in this category. Still, you may find more often than not that you want to salvage your relationship with them. This is advisable because these bitches have a high success rate when it comes to transcending.

Same Bitch, Different Name Bitches (if there were a planet full of clones, they'd live on it)

These common types of bitches seem to spew the same amount (and the same kind) of venom and are often found in your everyday life. Places like the gym, the post office, the airport, or your local bar are examples of this bitch breeding ground. These bitches can make life difficult, but usually you don't interact with them closely or for very long lengths of time. Kind of like a one-stop bitch shop. You may find yourself asking, "Really? Is this person *really* behaving this way?" These types can be obnoxious by themselves, but in the hierarchy, I find them collectively boring because their bitchiness is so predictable. You want to force-feed these bitches three shots of espresso and thoroughly make them chew red hot chili peppers so they'll shake things up a bit with their bitchiness. I mean, if you're going to be a bitch, then at least stand out—be different! Not more bitchy—just different. Where's my jar of peppers when I need it?

As far as transcending goes, it depends on the situation at hand. Nine out of ten times, you simply have to deal with these mundane souls while passing through the situation or environment, but there's room for relationship growth as long as they're more interesting as friends than they are as boring cloned bitches.

Li'l Bitches (annoying as a housefly, but they go away)
These are bitches that have mild forms of personality malfunction; they're more annoying than harmful. Their bitch tendencies usually aren't constant—the characteristics come and go and aren't ingrained in their psyches. What's more, Li'l Bitches are heavily influenced by environment or atmosphere, making them great candidates for transcending. If you had a fly swatter, you wouldn't necessarily want to swat to the point where their corpses were smashed against your sliding glass door. You'd simply swat them out of your door and lock it shut. Li'l Bitches absolutely can cross the line—don't forget: they do have bitch qualities. With these types, you need to have a box of holistic chill pills with you because they can be so annoying that you want to spike your Dr Pepper with Draino out of frustration. But not all Li'l Bitches are *that* bad—and even if they are, there's hope yet, as they don't know they're annoying. And that's where you step in and defuse rather than swat.

Big Bad Bitches

Player Haters

On-the-Job

Boob Envy

Hit-and-Run Male

Jack-in-the-Box

Single White Female

Floater

Player Haters

A Player Hater is a person who is insanely jealous of others, possesses an evil eye, and suffers from low self-esteem. A monkey wrench in society, the Player Hater has a false belief that life is a race or a game. This person possesses a deeply lodged notion that someone, hopefully he or she, will emerge the winner of this Great Game of Life. This mentality is borderline delusional in the sense that life really isn't a game—it's a gift. It's also delusional in the sense that the poison of hate has clouded these people's minds, making it difficult for them to trust others and not envy them. If they are overachievers, it's likely they're used to being ahead of the race and possess a certain degree of ambition and determination.

Player Haters will hate different people for different reasons, but one thing is clear: once they discover something about others that makes them feel threatened, inadequate, or inferior, then the game begins. Since Player Haters love to think in terms of games, any small challenge at which they can defeat you will suffice. A round of poker, pinball, or even rock-paper-scissors during lunch break can satisfy their competitive cravings. In addition, they may try to trap you into making bets with them because they enjoy being know-it-alls. What's even more twisted about Player Haters is that aside from living to beat you, they also get a thrill almost losing to you.

If you're friends with a person you suspect is a Player Hater, pay attention to the times when you're on that person's turf—for instance, while riding in the person's vehicle. It can be an all-out ambush when that person has total control and you don't. If you love a song on the radio and this person knows it, he or she may gab on the phone and turn the volume low. Or the person may purposely play music you don't like. The best thing is to do is to keep cool and store the incident in your mental Rolodex—it can be used later as a point of reference.

If you notice this subtle competitiveness, you'll find that it's often easier to let the person win—anything to stop the hate. And while many of them like to be in control on an intellectual level, there are those who hate on a physical level. When it comes to Player Haters, if they feel you have anything better than they do, then draw your sword! There's no reason greater for the evil eye other than jealousy of physical beauty, but life achievements or being popular in social circles can bring it on as well. Because the evil eye is a negative force that harms both the person sending it and the person receiving it, you should strive to avoid envy from all angles. It just so happens that as far as Player Haters are concerned, the hate usually starts with envy.

If you find yourself purposely dressing down and hiding under hats and glasses, you know what I'm talking about. I know a few girls who live in a state of fear because of player hating! In fact, one of them is filing a law suit because her coworkers' jealousy made her work environment a living hell. So many women get evil stares due to jealousy, and it's derived from low self-esteem on the Player Hater's part.

These self-esteem issues force these people into a competition mode. While they obsess over themselves, they also obsess over everyone else. It works one of two ways: either they are obsessed with themselves and hate anyone who poses a threat to them or they are obsessed with other people and hate them because they want to be like them. In worst-case scenarios, they can be a gnarled ball of both.

It's up to you to decide if you're dealing with a Player Hater or not. The bottom line is that if you are dealing with one, you must let the person go. Until Player Haters come to terms with themselves and unlock their hearts, they'll never be free of their deeply rooted issues. If you stick around without paying attention to the clues, you could suffer from disappointment when these people backstab or use you.

If you do have an encounter with a Player Hater, try to avoid conflict. These people can be boisterous, loud, and sometimes so overbearing that it's easier just to get the hell away. I'm currently referring mostly to teenagers since bitchy characteristics emerge for the first time around junior high. Mouthing off verbally to a bully can cause physical fighting or a trip to the principal's office, or both. Growing up, I was sent to the principal's office a lot, usually to "resolve some issues" with other girls my age.

On numerous occasions, I'd sit patiently in Principal Walker's office, waiting to be bombarded by hormonal teens experiencing acute "hateration." Mr. Walker knew I was a good kid and wasn't fazed by their *Jerry Springer Show*–like performances. They usually didn't last long—once they'd spewed out their frustration, we'd return to class without shit being resolved. But that *craving* was satisfied, and the hate continued well into my high school years. In fact, the hate never stopped. It was stressful at times, and that's why it's vital that the Inner Bitch be strong.

In retrospect, when I mentally journey back to Mr. Walker's office, I realize that I saw the big picture even way back then. I decided it wasn't worth the hassle to be mouthing off to the Haters all the time, and I found it irritating to miss class over their bullshit nonsense.

The first basic rule when it comes to identifying a Player Hater is looking for the subtle clues. Once it's determined that the person is being a Player Hater, you must then try to determine why he or she is hating you. Once you extract the cause for the hate, you can better assess what to do next. The next natural step would either be to attempt to transcend the Hater or let your Inner Bitch take over. Be warned, however, that attempting to transcend is a huge risk.

In an attempt to defuse and transcend, you're going to be required to be blunt with these bitches. Coming straight out and asking what exactly their problems are with you is the easiest way to avoid beating around the bush, and it will put them on the spot. Deep down, you should know already that the problem is lack of self-esteem and jealousy toward you, but confronting such people will make them take a good look at themselves. They won't be able to answer why they have a problem with you, because they're not going to admit that there's underlying envy.

The key ingredient in the recipe of success is your own Inner Bitch. With Player Haters, shutting the bitches down is the best way to handle them. As mentioned in the first part of the book, shutting down bitches stops them in their tracks. Be prepared in advance with what you want to say, what you'd like to say, and what you're going to say to the Player Hater. Unleash your lion! Keep your distance physically when verbally shutting them down because voices tend to rise with these types. I would also manage to have the confrontation in a place where you won't embarrass yourself in public but not risk them physically assaulting you at the same time. Player Haters are crazy, and when they are jealous and full of hate, pure rage can ensue.

The other option is simply to avoid them at all costs, although there is always that chance you will interface and an altercation will come about. So be prepared. Choose your words wisely but don't be afraid to tell these people off completely. Be certain what you're shutting them down about and back it up with specific examples so that they can't retort that you are grasping at straws. Be concrete, confident, and strong in your words—and shut 'em up!

Player Haters often have multiple siblings, so their need to compete for attention is greater than most people's. While it's possible to engage in healthy competition with these types, it's important not to lose sight of what you're competing for. These bitches set their standards high and don't like to wait for results. They want the results immediately, and they want things their way. Those who interfere or steal the spotlight are setting themselves up for a whirlwind of hate. Not only do Player Haters zero in further on the prize, but they also zero in on you. For a moment there, it was a cool game of darts but guess what: now you're the bull's-eye.

Once your Inner Bitch begins to blossom and you shift into new energy, Player Haters' cages will be rattled. They'll *smell* the new bitch in you and automatically hoist themselves on their high horses. Around others, they'll often be flamboyant, loud, or commanding. They may also murmur or engage in mindless chatter with others to make you feel isolated, as if to suggest no one is listening or paying attention to you. If you decide to take them on, they'll stay home and scrape their claws on the carpet until the showdown. Don't be intimidated. Once you see it for what it is, you'll begin to see that it's a compliment in a nutshell. After all, they wouldn't behave so bitchy if they weren't threatened by you.

The Player Hater is driven by the agony of defeat and will fight to the end. Suddenly, it's not about the promotion alone. It's about the promotion *and* beating your ass in the process. We do not want to carry this type of attitude. We all want the promotion because we worked for it, and while we can triumph over the fact that no one else obtained it, we can't let hate or revenge be the sole motivation for our actions.

One more factor that I think is worth mentioning when it comes to Player Haters is that they often have what I call a Scrappy-Doo of a friend. Going back to childhood cartoons, Scooby Doo's younger cousin Scrappy was always causing mischief and more trouble than good on the show. Player Haters often have Scrappy-Doos because they're extensions of the original bitch—they're little sidekick shits that are often as difficult to detect as the Player Haters themselves. While they have more bark than bite, it doesn't stop them from scheming, scoping, and watching you, even when the Player Hater isn't around. It's not uncommon for there to be more than one Scrappy-Doo, so watch your ankles.

In extremely rare instances, a Player Hater will be transcended and you can move on to a platonic, if not meaningful, relationship. Don't count on it but know that it's possible. When Player Haters are transcended, it's always by their will and has nothing to do with you. A life change or an epiphany of some sort makes them change for the better. They become satisfied with themselves and face their inner demons once and for all. Once they conquer that feat, they're free to enjoy relationships with others sans the hate. They must endure a completely personal journey before they can be transcended, thus making them the most difficult bitches of all.

If they're unable to be transcended, then you must cut them out of your life as quickly and painlessly as possible. There's no guarantee it'll be painless, but the rate at which they disappear will be more in your control. This is because the more wisdom and strength you gain, the easier it will be to unleash your Inner Bitch and discern who is and who isn't a helpful addition to your life. Once you've ejected Player Haters, it's likely they will develop a chips on their shoulders when it comes to their opinions of you. They may develop disdain for you, but take heart in knowing that their negative energy is directed somewhere else.

It's important to recognize unhappy people when you see them and know that certain negative circumstances are provoking their behavior. I advise patience and a calm attitude with such bitches because you aren't expected to change these people but tolerate them instead. If it becomes too unbearable at any time, you more than have a right to call on your Inner Bitch and stand up for yourself. The good news is that this is one of the only bitches that is a tough nut to crack transcend-wise. In fact, they're so stubborn that I wouldn't even recommend going out of your way to see eye to eye. Be as tolerant and patient as possible, turning your energy to people who are more receptive, compassionate, respectful, and understanding.

On-The-Job

I know this is something that we *all* have dealt with and will continue to deal with. What makes On-the-Job Bitches (OJBs) unique is that we don't have a choice but to deal with them. At their most offensive, they are upper management and can write you up—or worse yet, fire you.

Most executives don't have time to pick on their employees constantly. They are busy people, and problems at work reflect on them too. It certainly sucks when you have a boss you don't like, especially if that person is on a power trip and exercises it like no other. The person may flex his or her muscles by giving you extra workloads, more difficult workloads, and more responsibility than other coworkers got. This is especially true if the person simply doesn't like you or plays favorites. A negative relationship can affect you if you want extra time off, vacation time, or a day off, for the ones who are liked better may want the same thing at the same time. You may also get the shaft when it comes to lunchtime or break schedules. Some OJBs may not like anyone, while some may just not care for you in particular. You can't expect everyone to be like peas in a pod all the time, but there are certainly measures you can take.

When it comes to upper management, it's comforting to know that you may only interact with them at meetings or performance evaluations. You've really made a breakthrough when you can give a shrug and say, "That's my boss. Many people dislike their bosses. I'm normal." While you may not like the person, one tactic is to get the bitch to like you. People in upper management, no matter which level, have the guilty pleasure of knowing they are higher on the ladder than you are. They may not always admit it, but it's something they are extremely proud of. They wear an *invisible* badge of honor that they cherish immensely.

They rise in the morning, eat their Wheaties, and brush their teeth. They comb their hair and then pin on their imaginary badges, which gleam back at them in their mirrors. They position them, admire them further, and then send themselves big wet ones via reflection.

Be conscious of this imaginary badge. When you see your boss or supervisors, make it a point to see their imaginary badges. Get creative. Are theirs red, blue, periwinkle? Are they decorated with shapes, gemstones, or flowers? Do they say something? If so, what do they say? The point of this exercise is to acknowledge and remember that these people's certain perceptions about themselves are what allowed them to obtain the positions they're in. They don't forget about their badges, and neither should you. Actually, you should acknowledge the crap out of them. There are several ways to obtain their affection, in no particular order. The choice is yours.

First, whenever possible, ask the OJBs how long they have been working there. I think no matter how long it's been, this is a good response: "Wow! That's impressive/cool/outstanding that you hold such a great position." Let that be a starter for probing. This is Communication 101, people, and I want you to get an A plus! If these people have been working there forever and a day, or are just shy of that, you might say, "Wow! That's great you've been so committed/dedicated/loyal. We're lucky to have someone around who's so experienced with the company!"

Convince yourself you mean it. As cheesy as it sounds, it'll work if you sound like you mean it. This opens the door for them to do what people do best: talk about themselves. Just listen, nod, blink, and give the occasional "Mmhmm" (but do it quickly and not too often, as it's a verbal interjection and may subliminally irritate them).

Beyond this, a tactic with a high success rate, which I use all the time, is called the "double right." Let's say, for instance, they are prattling on about how they became employed with the company and what they did at first. Whenever they say something that gives an explanation (a supportive sentence), give them the double right.

For example, suppose its break time for the bitch. You sneak a quick bathroom break (hey, when you gotta go, you gotta go!) and pour some coffee in the break room, waiting for the person to arrive. You then hand him or her the coffee pot/mug/sugar and say, "Whew, my eyeballs needed a break from that computer screen! Sometimes I don't know if they'll pull through. You know, I am curious: You always seem so together and with it—how long have you been with the company?"

The bitch may give you a glare, but as he or she pours, a slight grin will appear. "Oh, well, two years, but I've been in the business for almost eight."

You nod. "I see. I was gonna say you must have an impressive history if it was something along the lines of that. But I wasn't sure—even if you had been here thirty years, you definitely are good at what you do."

The bitch's badge gleams. "Well, you know it's hard work, but I have a high work ethic."

"Where were you before you were hired here?"

"In Chicago. I was an administrative supervisor for the president of Total Bitch Inc. I was overseeing trainees."

You pause. "I see."

Give it a moment or two. One-one thousand, two-one thousand, three-one … Yes! The bitch's mouth is opening!

"I actually worked there for five years. When the opportunity for this company came along, the position was a lot higher, so I didn't hesitate."

"Right, right."

The person could have stopped at "overseeing trainees." The small silence gives him or her a moment to reflect. The bitch will subliminally expect another question. When you don't ask it, 90 percent of the time, he or she will volunteer more information. If not, it's most likely because you didn't really mean it so you sounded as if you didn't mean it. The Inner Bitch is somewhat theatrical, so have fun and pretend you mean it!

In this case, the supportive sentence I speak about is the one explaining how the bitch came to be at his or her current status. All you're doing with the double right is accepting the explanation verbally. This move will make you more likeable to the person. If the person has a lot of energy, you may want to ask how he or she conjures. Is it diet? Yoga and Pilates? Coffee? I'm sure the bitch would love to explain.

Zoom! There the bitch goes on a rampage about himself or herself, full of explanations and supportive sentences. It's a double right lover's dream when it comes to this fabulous conversation starring him or her, right over a freshly brewed cup of Folgers. Just keep up with the nods and the blinks, and anytime the bitch defends himself or herself, gives an explanation, or subliminally asks for your support, meaningfully chime in "Right, right."

Let's play a little more and go back to our supposed conversation. The OJB has now established how he or she got there, you gave a double right or two, and the person is still talking.

"So you know, I really love what I do, though at times it can be trying," the bitch says.

"Right, right."

"I do what I can and try to manage a home, a family." A sigh and furrowed brow are given.

"Totally! Most know how that can be, but it must be such a challenge being in the position that you're in."

At this point, these bitches will be so engorged in the statements of doing what they can when they can (boohoo) that they are thankful for your quick agreement and support. This buys you time so you can finish gracefully by saying, "But you know what? Better someone like you in charge who has the leadership skills!"

Priceless! The imaginary badge will gleam and shine. You've set this bitch up on the right path for the rest of the day. The beauty about this is that you have lost nothing. Actually, you killed three birds with one stone: you used the bathroom, grabbed some coffee, and took an extra step in making your boss love you! Get the person really talking for an admirable length of time and you've just cheated the clock. Kudos for you! I know that in general it's not wise to cheat the time clock, but let's be real: if you're buttering up the boss and the person enjoys it (which he or she will), you are winning because the OJB won't care if you're working on your silly papers. You are looking at the boss and admiring the badge! You're going to want to end the conversation, but if the person continues, by all means listen.

To close the conversation, you may want to say something like this: "I'm so glad I had the chance to talk to you! I have to return to my desk to get those files finished." If you want to take it a step further, you can add, "It's been refreshing." Refreshing indeed. Breathe in the office air and convince yourself that this isn't hell with fluorescent lights! It's all in the attitude, the approach, and the willingness to admit and accept that this person is your boss. You have some power when you make it a point to see the bitch's badge.

Going back to the example conversation, you are just probing to get these people to open and speak, which they usually will. As I said before, it is every person's nature to willingly talk about himself or herself. That's why this works so well. You, on the other hand, have a reasoning for engaging in such banter.

It's to your benefit; otherwise, you wouldn't give two shakes of a rat's ass. You'd be off somewhere talking about yourself! The whole universal truth of it lies in the fact that everyone, including you and me, has motives that are selfishly driven. If you don't buy this philosophy, treat yourself and read some Sigmund Freud. The man makes some good points. Just let go and let your inner bitch *relish* in the fact that you set out for this conversation and got it!

Timing is crucial so never approach OJBs after they've just blown someone's ass out of the water. Nor do we approach on Friday after work, when they're scrambling for their Audis. Break time, lunchtime, in the elevator—perfect! Also, on a side note, why not bring in a top-of-the-line sushi lunch one day? Do you fancy a morning break? Great! Waltz in there with fresh scones. There's nothing wrong with casting a little bait if you have a big fish.

I promise you this: if you let these bitches talk about themselves while you employ the double right, you'll have set the pace for a marathon of admiration. But remember, even though you normally wouldn't care what they say, there is more involved than just your verbal chimes. You don't necessarily have to care; I'm not gonna go that far. But you do have to *listen*. I know, I know—listening sucks! It demands our attention, our minds, and our memories. Just the thought alone makes us want to gag. But it shouldn't.

I will admit that I took a class in college called Listening. I got an A somehow. The last thing I did was listen, and that's if I even showed up! I didn't learn much, but I learned that listening is a powerful tool. Not many people know how to do it so they don't. That's why birthdates, names, and most little facts are lost in our minds almost immediately upon reception. If you take the time to listen, you can extract facts about the bitches that are memorable, important to them, and useful. Useful for what? For later conversations starring them, of course!

So let's role-play again and pretend that this bitch mentioned that he or she worked in Chicago for Total Bitch, Inc. Later that week, the bitch sees you and instantly says hello because, after all, you listened and opened the gates of flattery. You enthusiastically wave and walk over to the OJB and the accompanying imaginary badge. Meet the person halfway if possible. If the bitch wants to speak to you first, you'll know because he or she will have already started. If not, the bitch will be darting toward you with a zest of energy when you chime, "Oh my goodness! Aren't you a breath of fresh air today?" This will be received this with an overwhelming sense of gratitude.

"Oh, well, thank you and good morning," the OJB replies.

Turn it back to the bitch: "Good morning to you! Care for a morning treat? I have fresh scones."

If the bitch has time, fantastic. You'll impress him or her with such a wonderful assortment that something will be sure to fancy. If there is no time, fine. Just smile and say, "Oh, I don't doubt you're busy! While people like me can take the time for a scone, you've got an office to run! Better you're here than Chicago … I get no organization at home; thank goodness I get it somewhere!"

The bitch will love it! Not only have you offered a morning treat and flattered the crap out of the person, but you *also* threw in Chicago—a detail that is so pertinent because it showed you were listening. Listening equals caring. Caring about what? The OJB's little trip down bitch lane.

Flattery can take all different forms. If the OJB is really into fashion, when you create his or her imaginary badge, you might imagine it as a designer badge. Think Chanel's intertwining Cs or a shiny silver badge with the Tiffany & Co. label on it. If your OJB is a slave to fashion, it will be directly reflected in the choice of wardrobe. These bitches are very tailored, possibly St. John or Armani, and are always accessorized. Great fabrics, great shoes (always coordinated and well taken care of), great jewelry (for men, a tie or nice watch), and a great fit are standard protocol. These bitches have their shit tailored to a T because doing so amplifies and outlines them. It does nothing more, nothing less. And usually there is a flow of style. Fine knits, silk, and quality cuff links or scarves complete a nonchalant but oh-so-impressive ensemble. It's probable they enjoy their jobs more because they get to wear such great garb.

If you find you are working for a die-hard fashion fanatic, your best bet is to compliment the OJB on his or her clothing. It's a great way to get on the person's good side, but just be sure know what you're complimenting. You can't just stroll up and say, "Wow! Those are great shoes!" The bitch may be snooty and snide and quip "Thanks" while thinking, *I know, you idiot.* In order to compliment this person, patience pays off. Study him or her, keeping a log of what the person wears for a month, then do your homework. You'll find some consistencies, such as a favorite necklace, a preferred tie, or a pair of shoes that seem to go with everything. What you want to do is single out a piece and be sure you choose your favorite so your comment will sound sincere!

Vending machine/lunch break:

"You know, I just have to compliment you on your shoes! They are so flexible and go with so many things!"

"Oh, thank you," the bitch replies, clearly still uncertain at what you're driving at.

"I mean, they're extremely attractive. But what I like is that you can dress them up or down …" (Or wear them with black or white, blah, blah, blah.)

The person begins to open up. "Oh, yeah. I can wear them anywhere. It makes things easier!"

"Right, right. They look great. Are they pretty comfortable?"

The answer will likely be affirmative. If this person is truly a fashion freak, then he or she will wear designer, which is typically comfortable. Designer shoes are usually made in Europe and are of the finest materials.

Never, ever ask, "Where did you get them?" This is a pointless, stupid question because more than likely they're from somewhere like Neiman Marcus, Saks Fifth Avenue, or the designer store itself.

Never ask how much something cost. This is tacky and rude. You don't want to ask this, because when it comes to designer things and the people who buy them, price is no issue. If it is, it still isn't discussed because price shouldn't be an issue. Even if it's not to them, your asking makes it an issue to *you*. This breaks the fluidity and the common ground you are trying to establish. Don't go against the grain.

Never ask if the item is a real one, whether it's a handbag, watch, or so on. I hope I don't have to explain that one.

If you're fortunate enough to know ahead of time what label the piece is, or anything about it, say so! If the person's clothes have Chanel or Louis Vuitton logos all over them, then you have a cheat sheet. You can do a little background check and bust out with some impressive information. Establishing common ground is critical. To go a little further with some ideas, let's consider bosses who always smell of a certain scent. If their scents stink or aren't appealing, then obviously that's not their forte. Pick something else. But if a scent works or is totally claimed by your boss, compliment the OJB. Try to find out what scent it is and then impress him or her with your skills. When passing by, happily chirp, "My, my, my! You smell wonderful! Tell me: is that Eternity by Calvin Klein?" The compliment will be appreciated.

By the way, it is always a good idea to smell delicious yourself. Studies show that people who smell good and wear fragrance have higher rates of being viewed as not only more attractive but more intelligent as well. In addition, always be presentable and well groomed. Know that it's not totally for others; it's for yourself too! Make life easier for yourself and know that the more people like you, the easier your job can become. I don't think anyone can argue with that. Just think: if people like you, they'll want you to like them, and before you know it, you'll be answering questions about yourself!

Coworkers

Okay, so we think that we have only been sentenced to eternal damnation with our bosses? Think again!

On-the-Job Bitches can also come in the form of coworkers. How does one deal with a coworker? First, not all coworkers are created equal. Coworkers can be totally cool and also be your allies. They can serve as support teams and provide shoulders to cry on. They can display the same sorrowful looks when you're all swamped in mundane tasks.

Just because a bitch is your coworker doesn't classify that person into some special bitch category. You can have a Buyout Bitch coworker (someone to vent to over the lunch you paid for) or a Meet-You-Halfway Bitch (someone who listens halfheartedly about how you need more time for your presentation, agrees it's unfortunate, and then moves on to him or herself).

The worst-case scenario would be a player-hating coworker. What you have to be careful of on the job are the Player Haters. It's quite likely you will interact with others on a regular basis while at work, and while you may get along with most, every now and then you get a rotten apple.

In our private lives, we have the luxury of choosing those with whom we want to spend our time. When we're at work, we are forced to not only interact with others but *tolerate* them as well. You already may be good friends with someone at work. If this union has already occurred and been established, then fine. Just don't ever volunteer or sign up for any group assignments or buddy work.

You may conclude that by being buddies, you can chat over wine, do your project after the kids have been put down, or picnic at the beach over champ and straw and you'll excel to the highest level. Bless your hearts! What I love about this concept is that it is so sincere, so sweet, and so genuine. That is, until suddenly the deadline is fast approaching and neither of you has really produced anything up to par. You can be flustered and pray the other person will be ingenious and come up with something remarkable, but that person may be praying the same of you! Put in even more time restraint and before you know it, you start questioning if this person knows anything. If any more time restraint is added, then you'll find yourself scrambling to save your own ass by getting the spreadsheets and PowerPoint done. At best, you end up at the threshold of mediocre.

Friendships with coworkers cannot only demolish relationships but your career as well. In college, I used to loathe group projects. I preferred to do the projects by myself because at least then I knew that shit was going to be done right, effectively, and more than just the bare minimum. It was my grade and my reputation. I always expected to get stuck with the types of bitches who just coattail ride on hard work. To be honest, I never gave two hoots. It was better that way because I knew we'd do it my way and earn a better grade.

Classic bitch story: When I was a junior in college, I was two credits away from fulfilling my major. One of the final credits was a class called Interviewing. Fantastic! Who doesn't want to be a better interviewer or interviewee? I love interviews. They're often a great opportunity to work your magic, try out some reverse psychology techniques, and don that new interview suit. (In my professional opinion, you should go on as many interviews as you can! Even the ones that technically don't matter have something to offer. Even more than opportunities, they're *experience.)*

So there I was, a junior at my university, with a plan that after that semester, I would have a totally laid-back yet hard-earned senior year. It would consist of two dance classes, two creative writing classes, and one class on death and dying. I didn't show up a whole lot to the interviewing class, but I blame that on the time the class met and the teacher's lack of charisma.

The semester was ending, and I was riding on a very shaky C-. We were given ... ta-da—a group assignment. *This could work*, I thought. That thought was shot down faster than a Thanksgiving Day turkey when it was announced with whom I'd be working. I didn't have any biases, but they were three boys attending the biggest party school in America. They were nice boys, cool ones too. But because I'm not a fool, I knew these "coworkers" were really nothing of the sort. Even if we actually spent time putting our chronically clouded craniums together, I never would have passed. No way.

The infamous assignment was as follows:

> You are to present a topic relatable to students on the campus that poses a series of questions, perceptions, and values that can be measured through a series of assumptive questions (direct and indirect, as well as non-direct) on said topic. These findings will be condensed and represented by theory statement, evidentiary findings, and the drawing of conclusions. One final conclusion to said topic will be defended through the execution of questionnaires, the formal interviewing of subjects, and finally, the creation of no less than two focus groups concerning said topic.
>
> **Point worth: 350 points = 1/4 final grade**
> Due date: Tuesday, November 28, 2002

The fact that it was due the Tuesday after Thanksgiving break was a forewarning of trouble. We had nothing to go on. We had no clue as to what our topic would be, should've been, or could've been. We had discussed it briefly before class, toying with certain topics that these boys had suggested. Before I could even absorb their energy and refute their silly ponderings, I took matters into my own tentacles.

As "coworkers," we were supposed to be a team. I wanted to be kind and cool, but I knew I couldn't let kindness sabotage our grades. We went out a few times to lunch in an effort to brainstorm and figure out what our presentation would be. These lunches were a waste of time because being sweet and trying to decide who would do what within our assignment over a nice Wiener schnitzel was not in my deck of cards. I could see purely and simply that these coworkers were not going to contribute anything worthwhile to our work—the vibe was as if they knew I would be the boss and pull the weight.

That Thanksgiving, instead of going home, chowing down great food, and experiencing a wonderful day of football, I stayed on campus. I literally was in the campus library's basement with the dust mites for hours on end. I remember the shelves had these funny cranks on the ends of them, and when turned, the shelves would break apart, revealing more dusty books. And dust mites.

By the time I emerged from the depths of Strozier Library, the day had gone, come, and gone again, but I couldn't have cared less. What I had in my small hands was a huge accomplishment: the perfect presentation and thesis paper. It was the perfect length, the perfect font, had the perfect bibliography, and content that superseded any project I had ever spit out before, especially under such a time constraint.

Under the pressure, I had to completely come up with our thesis, but I also fabricated the evidence as well as the books we supposedly read (I was quite creative when it came to the titles). Furthermore, I totally fudged fake questions with fake answers that our fake foci groups gave (consisting of fake students, of course!)

It was insane. But my Inner Bitch was *not* about to fail due to a poorly timed class taught by a boring professor (who had me working with the presidential candidates for the Don't Do Shit Campaign.) Making the grade meant graduating on time. I had never been dishonest in school and never was thereafter, but the project was done straight from the heart because there was no other option. When those "coworkers" returned on Tuesday, they almost melted to the floor when I told them the report was finished. The scene was priceless. I felt good handing them my project because I knew it was quality work.

I handed one of the boys the intro and said, "Read this." I handed the other the conclusion and said, "You read this." I presented the ten pages in between. I did this because we had to *present* it, and I was the only one who knew jack shit about what was happening. They contributed nothing. We rocked that day by kicking the crap out of the other groups. That was not the goal, but it was certainly an extra plus. We scraped the bowl of a perfect score and walked away with an A flat (on an A+ scale.) The boys praised me nonstop, and though I haven't seen them in sometime, I will always be known as "the girl they wouldn't have graduated without." Aw—how sweet!

This may seem like a charming little fairy tale, but guess what. I didn't give two shits about those boys and what they couldn't do. I was looking out for myself, as should you.

Coworkers are an interesting lot because you should strive for an amiable relationship yet not get too close. You may think that they hear you out and feel all your pain but give them the chance to be promoted and they'll leave your cheese in the wind. Even if they have loved you, cherished you, or wanted to marry you, never join forces to get work done or volunteer for a group project together unless you're required to. You'll end up fucking yourself—and not in a good way. Mark my words. That's because for every Tweedle Dee, there's a Tweedle Dumb. It could happen to you!

Similar strains can occur in a relationship if you room with a friend. What you swore you could deal with you can't, and before you know it, you're avoiding each other completely due to some tension. Since we have ruled out very close friendships in the workplace, I assume that you know not to mix sex with your job. That can also end careers and certainly put strain on them.

Your work is a direct reflection of how ambitious you can be. Freud repeatedly stressed that ambition was one of the two motivations in life. Everyone possesses it, but there are those who follow their ambition closely, those who follow enough to get by, and those who don't do a damn thing with it. You need to view your work as a goal. View it as a piece of art in the making—a ladder to be climbed. Climbed for the sake of others? No! Climbed for the sake of yourself.

Take your job, whatever it maybe, and redirect yourself to make it as fulfilling and rewarding as you can. If you sincerely can't find fulfillment or rewards at work, you should get another job. Period.

If that doesn't sound appealing, dig deeper from within yourself. Don't settle! No matter how desperate you may be to find something likeable at your job, keep coworkers out of the choices. Be cordial but stay focused on your job. If you're friendly but keep to yourself, you'll decrease the chances of a coworker becoming clingy. In addition, be aware of any coworkers that constantly complain or have a gloomy outlook on life. Misery loves company so don't let them sink you too by listening to their job complaints and comparing them with yours. You can't save drowning people if they are drowning themselves! You simply don't have time. Disconnect yourself from them and connect yourself with higher-ups. Ambition, ambition!

The other problem that can occur with OJBs is when they don't like you and are tight with the boss. This automatically gives them leverage. Many times with these certain coworkers, it seems they don't do much of anything, while everyone else seems to do *something*. I wouldn't waste time complaining that these people get away with it. While it is certainly annoying and perhaps a little disgusting, it's not worth draining your energy while you dwell on it. You may find yourself doing extra around the office or the store (or any environment in which you work), so make certain that you don't allow these same individuals to coattail ride either. Make sure that if they are lazy, unmotivated, or militant, you don't conceal the problem. Don't dwell but don't conceal. I wouldn't exactly exploit it either, but I would suggest to these bitches ways that they can help out. Alternatively, you can ask how certain assignments of theirs are coming along. However, getting *your* job done is what really counts.

If you do encounter bitches at the workplace, remember that it's just work, and once you clock out at the end of the day, you've clocked the bitches out.

Boob Envy

If you have big boobs (real or fake), may I get an amen? Much like a Meet-You-Halfway, those with boob envy don't always want to hate you. They just hate that you have tits and they don't. The more time passes, the more I sympathize for Pamela Anderson. I know from the depths of my soul that that beautiful woman has repeatedly felt the slap of hate. She has seen hate in all shapes and forms. It must've been difficult for her at first, because not only are her breasts huge but they're also enhanced. Instant hate: just add saline. Haters took the fact that she had implants and wrote it off as some character flaw.

I have been asked, in terms of acting, if I think I will be labeled for having big breasts. Labeled as what? I don't know. Whatever it is, it's not keeping me from an acting career or my God-given right to a large rack. In the history of my boobs, I've been an A, B, and C before finally settling in a D. It wasn't as if my shit grew fast either. I was flat for a long time.

Female family members had more than enough, but mine were terribly shy, probably because I wanted them so badly.

It seems, though, that larger-busted ladies are subjected to much more hate, especially if they have implants. Women get the shit kicked out of them just for wanting to look more like women! And the shit is kicked from smaller-busted women because the au naturals have nothing to envy (they know they got lucky.) Hell, some want them smaller so let's look at and acknowledge the source. Small-busted women fall into three categories:

1) Small-busted and love their boobs
2) Small-busted and hate their boobs so they get implants
3) Small-busted and hate their boobs but are too broke or scared to go under the knife

If you do have implants, you're at an especially high risk of Big Breast Interrogation, in which you are pressed to answer a series of questions related to your "jubilees." This may occur in any social setting, and the chances are greater if there's alcohol involved. Boob Envy Bitches may get tipsy and begin to ask personal questions. Usually they'll ask your permission first so be skeptical if any of the following are posed to you:

"I was wondering if I could ask you something personal."

"May I ask you something personal?"

"Would you be offended if I asked you something private?"

"Can I ask you something private?"

There's no question about it: you are going to be asked if you have implants. You can stop the questions dead in their tracks by replying, "I'd rather you not." People have to respect this. Why should you suddenly put yourself in the position of being uncomfortable? There's no question about it, he or she is going to ask if you have implants. If you don't care about discussing it, then by all means proceed—just realize you've opened a can of worms (all over your chest.) The questions are usually rapid-fire, and there are some definite ones you can count on, such as:

"How much did the operation cost?"

"Who performed it? Was it someone local?"

"Was the surgery scary?"

"Where are your scars?" (This is the most offensive question of them all. What difference does it make to them?)

Some women are truly interested and simply gathering information. These girls aren't true haters;

they're just tacky. It's in poor taste to ask anyone about any surgeries or operations they've had, especially if cosmetic. It's an invasion of privacy, puts people on the spot, and is just downright uncool. Haters will ask these questions because it's in their nature to make you feel smaller. They may seize the moment and try to flatten your ego by drawing attention to the fact that your breasts are enhanced. Deep down, it gives them satisfaction because it reiterates that you thought your breasts were less than perfect—to the point where you went out and *fixed* your problem. Well, kudos to you! They'd do it too if they had the balls!

If you have small boobs and find that you hate women with implants, reread this chapter. Do something about it too! You can spend the rest of your life with or without tits—the choice is solely yours. If you want them, don't sit there and try to convince yourself that you don't. Treat yourself! If you ignore the urge to do what you truly desire, it'll haunt you forever. In the meantime, while you're still playing mind games with yourself, some other chick will be lying on the table about to join the world of plastic you've come to deny.

But bear in mind that if and when you do have surgery, you'll be subjected to hate. Sometimes it's easier to tuck breasts away under cardigans and turtlenecks, where they're safe from evil eyes. There are women out there who are angry at the world and angry at God for having none or little breasts. This hate played a role in my being struck in the face one night in Los Angeles. I knew why then, and I know why now. The same hater had her breasts done a little over a year later. She repeatedly pointed out that her implants were just a finger width apart when it came to cleavage. She damn well knew my valley is a particularly vast and wide one. Not surprisingly, I eventually let this bitch go for good.

No one can drink from the golden cup of life if it's tainted with the poison of jealousy. Boob Envy Bitches can be transcended only by surgery because their attitudes are derived from jealousy—housed in the home of a Player Hater. Don't poison your cup of life just because someone else's cups runneth over! Handle your jealousy, treat yourself to some tits, and raise your goblet for a toast. Here's to big plans, big dreams, and big boobies everywhere! Cheers!

Hit-and-Run Male

These bitches hit it and quit it the moment they think you want something more. Some men go overboard and give themselves way too much credit— this isn't unusual for a Hit-and-Run Male Bitch. Men are no strangers to commitment phobia, so some will bolt like lightning if they suspect you're developing feelings for them. There are instances when women really don't want anything more than just a "doo-wop" here and there, or so I tell myself. I think any girl sleeping with any guy can keep it casually cool as long as he does. *I think*. Of course, we're always open to spending more time with this hookup if he shows interest.

Luckily for us, male bitches can keep us from getting for the wrong person. They restrain us from taking a booty call from bed to dinner to movies to trips to Disney World to living together to the altar—yikes! Many times when we are on a roll with someone, we don't realize how much time is passing. My relationships have lasted obnoxiously long, just out of steadiness. My partners and I always had the best years for, like, three years, and then things would take a sharp turn for the worse. At the end of each, when I reflected, I realized I'd have to start being more choosy and less lenient. I didn't want any relationship if he wasn't top notch everything.

Although I told myself this, I still stubbed my toe and fell for my first bedroom buddy. I went through some emotional shit after he slammed the door in my face. He'll never know just how deep my wounds were. I'm sure some of you have been in love with someone and pined for that person for so long that when you finally got together—*kablam!* Your heart exploded into a mushroom-shaped cloud. However, with any male bitch, you have to be strong about your ego getting bruised and facing rejection. Take heart in knowing it's him, not you (don't you hate that shitty explanation?). I know it sucks, but in it rings a certain truth. It's not that you *need* or even *want* this Male Bitch. After all the pain, if he were to come crawling back with daisies in his hand and eyes full of tears, would you really want him? Perhaps, and you are free to exercise that right. But don't do it because you feel you've won this way. Male bitches don't really compute anything more than your taking them back. They're like babies. Babies know that when they cry, someone will comfort them. If you take a man back out of your own desperation for a companion, this is how he will compute that: *As long as I say I'm sorry, it will smooth over the situation.*

When my ordeal was happening, I was extremely upset and confused. How could he just run like that? I have learned that it's something male bitches do. And it hurts. I had my days where I ate pizza until I couldn't stuff one more pepperoni down. I sang Mariah Carey's "My All" in the dark, comforted only by a few candles. I cried, burned pictures of the guy, and imagined him walking out of my life wearing a red backpack.

All this helped, unbelievably, but I was in it for the long haul. I vowed revenge. I was going to be a star first, and even though I thought I'd never see him again, he would see me ... in bright lights on a big screen! Luckily for me, this energy propelled me forward for some time, and once I developed feelings of self-love, self-motivation, and self-righteousness, I stopped obsessing over how bad I was shit on and stopped caring. *Yes*, I told myself. *I had been shit on*. The pile of shit I was buried under was bigger than a Tyrannosaurus rex's. He threw me for quite a loop, and what he did was downright bitchy, no matter which way you dice it.

In all honesty, these bitches know they're being little bitches. In fact, they're such little bitches that they seek shelter under rocks. They know when they owe you an explanation and an apology. As time goes on, it just adds to their marathon on the trail of disappearance until it becomes so late in the game that they ask themselves, "Does it even matter anymore? Is it safe to come out or am I in trouble?"

Let's examine the first question: Does it even matter anymore? The length of time you knew the bitch before he upped and ran will determine whether it still matters. In most cases, the girl *will* find the strength to move on. She may be a little jaded (or very jaded for a shorter period), but eventually she will realize that life is better without the coward and will be swept off her feet by a soldier. As for the bitch in question, it will always matter. No matter what he tells himself, it will continue to linger.

People are born with the natural gift of choice and self-direction. We are also born with gut instincts. People use many quirky cop-outs to justify their actions, but their guts tell them they are not being just. Male bitches know when they owe you an explanation, so rather than pressing them for an explanation, just let them be. If you knew him for a short period, it is less likely that he will to resurface. Some guys may never come around. You can double the chances of a no-show if he is in the eighteen-to-twenty-four-year-old range or if any of the following applies:

- You were on spring break.
- You met him at a random club on a random night.

- You met him in Vegas or at the Playboy Mansion.
- He's married/has a serious girlfriend.
- He's in the military and has been deployed.

You may have been that little slipup or that little fling on a wild night. Enjoy it for what it was worth and let go. Think of your fantasy man as a guy like this but with more ethics. They're out there, and I am sure that when they're met in the right situation, the stage will be set for a possible romance.

The key is discerning the difference between a guy who is a potential partner for life and a guy who is a straight-up treat. Don't confuse the two and please don't twist them around. I was with a guy who was nothing like what I envisioned a perfect mate to be except that he was extremely attractive to me. While that sounds like a good start, it was still a shitty situation because while he was an interesting guy, he had no goals or overall life map. What made matters worse was that he beat himself up for no reason whatsoever and as a result was inconsiderate to others.

Yet sexual desire, as Freud would agree, drives us just as much as ambition. The difference? With ambition, we are solo, but with sexual desire, there is another participant. That leaves people vulnerable to rely on another for complete satisfaction. I had to gain control of myself and not drop everything for a quick doo-wop. It was hard because even though this guy was my complete opposite when it came to approaching life, we had such good chemistry in the sheets that I said at times, "Screw everything else. I *deserve* treats too." Bear in mind with male bitches that if they rocked your world in the sack, they may be even harder to let go of. Treat yourself by all means, but don't get treats mixed up with a partnership and don't let a bruised ego from a male bitch scare you from real men.

This leads me back to the story about the original male bitch. Where were we? Oh yeah, how could I forget? After my heart was splattered all over the floor like house paint, I went on with my life and thought of him less and less. When I did, it was usually because I saw his name imbedded in a billboard or when a particular song was played. Once I could actually sing along with such songs again without making the negative connection, I knew I was well on my way.

I finally met the guy who scooped my heart up and pieced it back together. Was the new guy a rebound? Hardly. The bitch was on his way out anyway. The new guy totally extracted the bitch from my mind. I was madly, insanely head-over heels in love and basking with newfound liberation. This guy was *it*, no questions asked. What was his problem? He had a girlfriend. I fell in love immediately, but even if you rebound a bit, it's quite all right. Rebounds aren't a bad thing—quite the contrary. A rebound is someone you land on and he helps you bounce back, like a trampoline. Does anyone prefer to keep falling? Hell no!

Use the rebound as strength. It's not that you don't like the person—sure you do. And it's not as if when you're all better, you'll just dump the person. The situation is pivotal in that you remain the same person, but you'll be moving forward in a different direction. This person can be a catalyst for helping to change and shape you on your journey to recovery. So don't say, "No rebounds, no rebounds." Take them, welcome them, and bounce away!

Let's go back to the question of whether it matters anymore. I'd bet a lot of money that their hit-and-runs will matter to most of these weasels. You'll enter his mind in some way, probably much the same way he enters yours: through songs, scents, or a simple thought. He might remember your birthday or see a restaurant that you never went to together (but he does remember you saying you were fond of it). Even if he doesn't remember these things, the bitch will still know he acted like a bitch.

As time passes, he may never make an effort to contact you. Because it won't get you anywhere, there's no sense wondering if he will. Just vow to never do the same to anyone else, and if you have in the past, take it as karma working its ways. The bitches that are ready to come around will do so because they need closure with themselves, and it begins with you.

After a year and some months, karma came back my way. After this dude finally met my best friend through serendipity, he contacted me through e-mail. He was friendly and kind, and most of all, he was man enough to finally put closure to the situation. He outright wrote that he was sorry, that I deserved more (better), and that it was wrong of him to run in the other direction instead of facing it head-on. We're all guilty of running from confrontation or admitting when we're in the wrong, so he salvaged any self-respect I once had for him. I appreciated his taking the time to admit he was a piece of shit back in the day. I appreciated all the things he wrote, but it wasn't anything I didn't know. However, it was closure to the Hit-and-Run Bitch. It felt good to at least see it in print, where I could read it over and over until I was overflowing with closure.

I admit that I relished in it at first. I toyed with the idea that after all that time, I was still on his mind. But I had to check myself when I found myself thinking, *What if we hooked up and went on a date, then movies and dinner, and then here comes the bride!* That's how quickly a woman's mind works; we shoot ahead faster than a light-year. If the outcome could possibly lead to marriage and a safe, committed union, then we're ready to talk second chances. Bear in mind, though, that just as boys will be boys, bitches will be bitches. Instead of running back into his arms or using the apology as a plea to take you back, recognize it for what it is and move on. There's always an underlying selfishness in every action we take as humans: he's trying to get the monkey off his back for his peace of mind, not yours.

Take the apology, maybe make a deal to be friends or at least be civil, but do not retrace your steps. You want to move forward, not backward. Leave the thought that he's a changed man for another girl and go get the man that you deserve. Better yet, let him get you. Again, you possess an Inner Bitch. Should you reach the point that you have no time for male bitches and their nonsense, it's perfectly acceptable to utilize the strength the Inner Bitch carries. It never hurts to remind him that bitch behavior on his part can result in extreme tragedy, as Cameron Diaz demonstrates with Tom Cruise in *Vanilla Sky*. Remind him of this only if you really want to rid yourself of the bitch, as he may be a little spooked.

So what happens down the road if you're considering another sexual encounter? Is it politically correct to give him the benefit of the doubt? That's up to you, but he'd better make it up—and then some. You should make that clear. He should strive to make it the most earth-shattering, mind-blowing experience you ever had. He should strive to make it ten times better than your previous experience, and you should let him know you weren't too impressed from the get-go.

If you decided to sleep with him again, a little pre-sex ego shattering isn't out of line. There's nothing in this world that can demolish a man's ego faster than when you state, "You didn't make me come." If you faked it before, go for the jugular and *tell him so*! You faked it—what is he gonna do, make you come now? Well, put your money where your ding-a-ling is, mister.

Put him to the test by asking this question: "You didn't make me come, so what's in it for me?" Hopefully his answer is (C): orgasm. I guarantee that 90 percent of the time, he'll take the Pepsi Challenge, but don't be fooled, because it's not for your sake. It's crucial to remember that these bitches are mostly concerned with themselves; you and your orgasm are simply by-products of the shattered egos they're trying to mend.

It's only worth a second round if you sincerely think it'll be worth it. After you beat him up a little, sound the bell and tell him to go see his ringside water boy right quick. Let him rehydrate, apply Vaseline to his wounds, and then come see about you. Male bitches will take this one of two ways: either they'll be knocked out and therefore bow out or they'll beat their gloves together and give it a go. Regardless, your punches will be brutal. Don't feel bad. The bitch had it coming.

If you're the modest type, you can say it more gently: "You didn't take me to town." He'll get the point. How you say it depends on your Inner Bitch. You don't have to sugarcoat it; it's okay to be frank. It's a great marvel that unless they are older than dirt, most Male Bitches just need a few good yanks, licks, or tricks and they're done. Women, on the other hand, are extremely mental. What's more, our anatomy varies from woman to woman, which makes the challenge even better. But *real* men, not bitches, enjoy this challenge. The concept goes back to the Neanderthals, and it's all about the chase, the trophy, the prize. The choice is yours but proceed with caution, as these are Big Bad Bitches that can really do a lot of damage to your feelings.

You are in control. He obviously has some ulterior motive, so you may as well have one too. Even if he did take you to town, tell him he didn't! He deserves a little ego shattering. After all, your ego was shattered for days, months, or possibly longer. You were left scratching your head over where he went and had to wonder if he met Christopher Columbus, became convinced that the earth was flat, set sail, and fell the fuck off the planet! I say let him stay off the face of the earth—if he wasn't smart enough to stay with you, let the jerk be gone. Bye-bye, slimy buffoon!

Jack-in-the-Box

The Jack-in-the-Box Bitch is reminiscent of being five years old. At some point, most of us have been presented a colorful box with a crank. It looks like fun—a lot like a treat. You crank the crank and are greeted by a pleasant musical tune. This keeps you intrigued, but in the flash of a second, you are thwarted, discombobulated, and completely shaken up by the eruption of a bullshit piece of plastic dressed up as, of all things, a clown.

There are a few key elements here. First let's acknowledge that Jack-in-the-Boxes are clowns. They are jokesters, pranksters. Do you know how many people are afraid of clowns? A lot. These bitches do what they do best by catching you by surprise. You are lured by the delicate tune, then *boo!* Out pops this scary person, made up in paint and unrecognizable. He or she is masked, just like a clown, and can downright scare the shit out of you. Who you thought was your friend suddenly isn't, and it's horrible in the sense that the person caught you completely off guard. Some things in life catch you off guard and are worth it. I'm talking marriage proposals and a fat rock, but not jokesters.

What separates these bitches from everyone else is that you have no preparation, no heads-up. But don't despair. There are explanations for this horrid behavior. One explanation is that the value they place on your relationship is relatively low. You weren't so close to begin with, so time spent together isn't really factored in. Classmates, neighbors, and coworkers are suspects for this category. Not terribly long after the connection is made, they jump out of their boxes and show themselves for what they are. They're over being politically correct, cordial, or tactful. They're self-absorbed and therefore blinded to the possibilities of a deeper connection.

Sometimes after being reintroduced or reunited with someone you knew formerly, the risk that the person is a JITB is high. You may recognize the traits shortly after a transition of physical placement—for instance, if one of you switches jobs/moves/changes schools and you're still in touch. These bitches adapt well to those around them, usually extracting what they need from individuals in order to progress further. They take from many souls, on many levels, so as far as they're concerned, they can take you or leave you. Don't fret if they leave you; be happy they are gone! Realize that it's the surprise that makes it painful because the people came across as cool on the surface.

I witnessed a firsthand account with a childhood friend and her JITB. My friend was visiting Los Angeles, and she caught up with a former classmate who was living there too. They went to lunch early Friday, and I ran into them at the supper club Friday evening, and although I'm a total vibes person, the first thing I thought when I saw this girl was "hairy." But since I'm nice and have tact, I overlooked the flaw and gave her the benefit of the doubt. I could tell by her eyes, however, that she was a bona-fide Player Hater. The situation was turned up a notch when I was introduced to her Scrappy-Doo, who, when it came to stature, was a pipsqueak.

It was a Barney and Baby Bop production, and although I immediately knew what I knew about them, they caught my childhood friend by surprise. The bitch "jack-in-the-boxed" it, complete with fries. And my friend had to leave with them because she arrived with them, so it was only polite for her to finish the night with them (I disagreed, but I guess it's the best of manners). The bitch didn't want to drop her at my house later that evening, and I felt sorry that my friend had to spend one more evening with them.

After all, they were Player Haters if I ever saw any. The Scrappy-Doo kept staring at my boobs before finally asking "The Question." I shut her down by saying, "Yes, they are real; and no, you can't touch them." Since she was still foaming at the mouth, I quipped, "You just can't get past Sandy and Mandy, can you?"

Since I have learned to control my sassy mouth and bring my knowledge of haters to a deeper understanding, I stopped there. I caught her stealing glances; she couldn't help herself. I really wanted to tell her never to wear faux fur again. I'm not saying to slay all rabbits, foxes, and chinchillas alive, but please don't wear an entire coat of some synthetic material posing as fur. Thank the good Lord above she wasn't carrying a faux Louis Vuitton too, though I don't doubt that's next on her fashion list.

That horrific error, matched with that synthetic attitude, made a weak impression on me. I concluded that she needed to be shipped away Fed-Ex style with no tracking number, as in *please get lost*. Anyone receiving her as a package would probably turn his or her nose up and slam the door. To this day, I've never seen such a blatant example of a Jack-in-the-Box Bitch. Just as we are discovering new forms of life on Earth, we were discovering a new type of bitch.

The faux fur offender was a prime example of a Scrappy-Doo, who is an extension of an original Bitch, as mentioned previously. They happen. If you haven't met one yet, you probably will. As unpleasant as they can be, you must take heart in knowing that you wouldn't pull such stunts. You are what you are (think Popeye), and such is a bitch to be frowned upon with disdain and utter disappointment.

Handle them with caution but with a significant amount of loss when it comes to your expectations and respect.

When it comes to bitches as such, they have tattered and torn the very fabric with which you regarded them in the first place. But don't be discouraged; that's what we have higher thread counts for. Slam the box shut, chuck it into the nearest Dumpster, and keep marching forward.

Onward and upward!

Single White Female

This is crazy (imagine that!), but I used to have two friends in a particular category that I really think watched the movie *Single White Female* way too many times. Just to inform you, in case you haven't seen it, I'll give you the nutshell breakdown: The movie is about a young woman named Ally who has a painful breakup and decides to get a new roommate to take her mind off it.

The new roommate, Hedy, having her own disturbed issues, is admiring and becomes obsessed with what seems like "the perfect life" that her roommate Ally has. Little by little, this crazy bitch starts wearing Ally's clothes, changing her hair so it was just like Ally's, flirting with Ally's boyfriend … It's all Ally, Ally, Ally. If it were nowadays, she'd be taking selfies and posting them on Instagram as Ally. Eventually, things spiral out of control, and in a very suspenseful ending … Well, let's not talk about the movie. Let's talk about the Single White Female Bitch.

The SWF falls into the most dangerous categories in the hierarchy. As with most Big Bad Bitches, they're very strong in the department of hate. Hate is a powerful emotion, and this particular bitch has hate, anger, wrath, jealousy, lustfulness, disdain, and envy all wrapped up in one nasty package.

That being said, repeat after me: psy-chot-ic. These terrifying bitches hate you and they hate what you have, but they want to be you and want what you have. What's worse? Often they just want *you.* This is the type of bitch that you will want to cut off completely.

Transcending is extremely difficult, if not impossible, because these individual are sick, but you can use the tactics I provide to remove them from your life and do so without making them go physically psycho. Here are key characteristics of a Single White Female Bitch:

- Stalking by calling or e-mailing more and more frequently based on lack of your response
- Prying into your life by asking you or others about what you've been up to and then trying to interject themselves in your social or professional setting
- Causing physical harm to you and/or your belongings

Realize you are at risk here. It's tricky business when dealing with a SWF bitch, but it can be done. When it comes down to the wire, the only one who can stop this bitch is you and that Inner Bitch of yours.

Let us start with stalking. With a SWF Bitch, there is a certain sort of "intimacy seeking" desire in order to develop a loving yet not always intimate relationship. This could include being BFFs (a.k.a. best friends forever) for life or a feeling that you both have life designs that include each other. I have had really, really good friends in my life, but through thick and thin, I only have *one* best friend. And she ain't either one of these SWF bitches, m'kay?

Phone calling, e-mails, hunting you down ... With one of them, I had to change my phone number. She still e-mails, but I have a gazillion different addresses now, and I only check the old e-mail to skim since it's so full of junk mail. Once I started to notice that my taste in clothes was being (literally) copied and the bitch was buying the same makeup (again, literally) and even using my same linguistics, which are mine and mine only, I started to raise a highbrow. When I couldn't find my favorite shorts (her knowing that I loved them and had pondered right in front of her as to their whereabouts), I stumbled across them in her drawer. Oh, and my favorite Chanel eye shadow. Sometime later, my favorite clip.

I noticed over time that despite my not knowing about all my personal effects missing (at the time), she was slowly almost morphing into a mini-me. Needless to say, as much as I wanted to believe this wasn't happening, it was. And it not only hurt me; it disturbed me. I cut the umbilical cord, and that was that. Cutting these bitches off is like a making a U-turn. You have to know when the right time is to turn and you do it gracefully so you don't just peel out and get hit by oncoming traffic. It's a delicate situation.

Prying is another aspect of the SWF Bitches. Remember, part of their characteristics is that they actually want to be you in a sense. That's why they are copycats through purchasing similar clothes (or in my instance, the exact same—the other one just took them), makeup, hairstyle, or whatever they can emulate. So once they have your look and can imitate you somewhat, they try to move into your social and professional circles. The way they achieve this is through prying. They start with people who they met through you. They find a way to see or phone them, drop your name as validation, and before you know it, they're meeting up with these people.

These bitches have a frame of mind that in their emulation and obsession of you, they look for loopholes to get closer to you (if you've distanced yourself or cut them off completely). If you're still friends, they start to emulate you in an effort to get closer to your circle professionally and socially. That is how these bitches operate. Major creep factor! I can't stand them!

Now, when it comes to physical harm of you and your belongings, this means that when you're hanging out, they may sabotage by encouraging you to eat unhealthy food, doing anything to excess (such as spending), convincing you that you don't need to exercise, and so on. They may also speak badly of your boyfriend and plant seeds in your head that he lies, cheats, or isn't worthy of you. These traits are physical harm that SWFs do to you.

She also may harm your belongings by being careless, such as dirtying dishes, spilling things on furniture, making a mess of your bathroom, borrowing clothes and not caring for them, and screwing up the controls on the TV remote "by accident." Bitch, please! Again, the best way to deal with these bitches is to make a U-Turn and go pedal to the metal for the hills. Cut off all ties, whatever it takes. Once you do that, do this: Tell others close to you about what you experienced with the bitch. Instruct them to not disclose *any* information about you to this bitch. Absolute zilch! Warn them to be wary of this bitch, as she is only using them to get to an obsession and could easily pose as a threat to them as well. Watch your booty in your professional circles by finding out (quietly) who she may have come in contact with.

When it comes to your professional circle, it's not wise to follow steps one, two, and three. But what you can do is have a warm conversation with some of your associates or affiliates and, being the fabulous you, casually question or say (while gently smacking the person on the arm):

> "Oh, you met Ms. Single White Female, didn't you?"
> "I heard you met Miss Single White Female recently …"
> "Yeah, yeah, Miss Single White Female said she spoke to you recently ……"

The answer will be yes, and at that point, you say, "Yeah, yeah, we're not friends anymore, unfortunately. She did some strange things. I don't *trust* her." Cue the crickets. If the person asks any more questions and presses you for answers, simply reply, "Well, we're in a professional atmosphere, so I'm not at liberty to discuss it, but in a nutshell? Watch out—she's toot-toot!" Circle your index finger around your temple, which basically indicates that that *bitch is nuts*, and leave it at that.

Floater

It's a fact that we all need to eat in order to survive, so we put food in our mouths and eventually use the toilet. Toilets were invented to flush waste away through some piping, where the waste was never to be seen again. Unfortunately, sometimes the waste refuses to be banished into exile, so it reappears and floats, forcing one to flush the toilet again. At the very worst, it causes an overflow, which wreaks havoc on all parties involved.

This analogy is *the ultimate* for Floater Bitches. Floater Bitches are one of the most dangerous bitches because they're hard to detect, thus making them so resilient. They refuse to be flushed, and if tampered with, they can easily cause chaos for a number of people. The reason they have such a large reach is because aside from their refusal to go away, they also "float" from one social scene to another. They often float back and forth from one clique to another in an attempt to gain approval from one side or both.

These bitches can appear in several settings: at school, a job, at PTA—you name it. Generally, whenever there is a social scene of some sort, you can be assured that there are some Floaters or two drifting about. They may get along with everyone and seem to have a genuine interest, but the only interest they truly have is keeping themselves viable. Seeking approval for them is important because they lack self-esteem.

Let's open up that thought for a moment. Let's talk about self-esteem and how it affects Floater Bitches. Obviously, they have zero self-esteem, because if they did, they would stand for something and be a leader, not a Floater. This is not to be confused with being a "follower"—some followers are so because they have low self-esteem and some because that's simply their nature. Nuh-uh—not with Floaters. Floaters can be clingy folk. They drift around until they find the group or person that gives them the attention and validation they so desperately desire, but they never shut the door on other possibilities because they will float on if need be in their quest.

You may think:

Oh, but they just want friends.
Oh, they just need others to talk to.
Oh, they're in need. I feel so bad.

Yeah, yeah, yeah. If you're a sympathetic type, great. There are so many edgy broads out there that I could have constructed a Park Avenue condo based on their shoulder pads alone. Don't be naive. You see, part of the Floaters' tactics is to seem innocent. The danger lies in their hidden ability to stir the pot. As I pointed out earlier, traveling back and forth from one person or clique to another is the Floater Bitches' specialty—it's their secret weapon, especially in closely knit social circles. Whilst clinging to one group before floating to another, they have the power to obtain a lot of data and (often) secrets of the party they currently are clinging to. Then, in an effort to gain attention from another clique or person, they float that information right on over until the other party is panting in curiosity over what secrets they hold—and vice versa.

There is an element of gossip within these bitches, which is a very bad trait. However, the Floater Bitches use it to their advantage to gain that approval and to restrain others. It becomes a sort of Ping-Pong game, to the excitement of the Floaters, because all of a sudden, their arms are being tugged left and right in a fight to get more information. Before you know it, you're at the mercy of the Floaters in an attempt to find out the truth. Depending on what information they have (and reveal), you may find yourself paranoid as well as suspicious about another party. Again, another important facet of the Floaters is the play of innocence.

Let's get one thing straight: Floaters are *not* innocent! That's why they're in the Big Bad Bitch area of the hierarchy. They may play innocent, but that's simply another tactic they use to obtain what they want. For instance, let's say you and a friend in your social circle have had some tension and the Floater is your "social something in common." After gaining your trust and your approval, you mention that particular "tension" friend. The bitch pries into why there is such tension. You don't necessarily spill the beans, but you throw a diamond encrusted bone or two about the situation into the air. The Floater Bitch catches said bone, floats on over to Miss Tension, and casually mentions you. Not any tension with you, just *you*.

Well my, my, my, what have we here? Um, yeah, it's called a setup. Your very name alone is likely to strike a nerve. Through what is seemingly just a little chitchat, a little "Oops, I farted while laughing during tea" conversation, just surface gab, a seed has been planted. One thing I know about certain bitches is that they are like a dam—they hold energy and emotions tight. And sometimes all it takes is a minor crack to break a dam wide open.

Because the Floater is that crack and little by little the dam of emotion begins to fall apart, the Floater will float on to another area of attack—a whole new breed of unsuspecting victims.

They will absolutely play the innocent card by saying things such as:

> "Oh, I didn't know *that* was what's going on."
> "Oh, I certainly didn't intend to offend either of you!"
> "This was *not* my intention."

Red flags. Do yourself a favor, and go to Bed Bath & Beyond (or wherever) and get yourself a red cloth of some sort. If you ever hear any of those words from another human being, please wave that red material in your face. Red flag. And if you can't do it for yourself, do it for me! *Thanks!* Know it's a red flag that this is a bitch not worthy of your time. M'kay? Great!

Okay, now for the good stuff: how do we handle such a putrid monstrosity? I'll be honest. When it comes to Big Bad Bitches, we're dealing with over-the-top behavior. It is disturbing. The Floater Bitches are the most disturbing because they are twofold: part just wants to float around in their own selfish need for acceptance, while the other part refuses to be flushed because of that same selfish need. Later in the book, I discuss the phenomenon that is a Binary Bitch, and the Floater is an applicable example.

The number one way to stop Floater Bitches is to discern exactly whom they are floating to (and trust me, they are floating to *someone*). The other party could be a friend, an acquaintance, an ex, or a stranger … *anyone*! The key is to (on the hush) find out who the Floater has been talking to or, better yet, influencing. Here are some key questions to consider when handling a Floater Bitch:

1) Who do you and the Floater have in common?
2) What is your current status with said Floater and his or her affiliates?
3) Is there any tension between any of the persons?

Once you have identified the Floater's target, you can simply reach out to the target and express your concern over gossip and rumors. It might be uncomfortable at first, but you have your Inner Bitch. Handle it. Handle the conversation (versus confrontation). Be direct. If you can't handle it, your Inner Bitch can. Listen, there is nothing in this world that can't be worked out or mended if it's true and just. And if you hold to your values and reach out beyond the Floater, beyond the gossip and the negativity, you will see a hand reaching out for you too. So ask questions and be bold!

I promise that the Floaters will see that their "innocence" is shattered once they see your Inner Bitch connect with the other party—and they will drift off into someone else's space. As far as you'll be concerned, it's into obscurity. And then you can work on your relationship with your "tension" friend—who probably is another bitch in this book. But in the meantime, imagine slamming down the toilet seat and thinking of the Floater as a piece of fecal matter that with just one flush goes *swish, swish, swish* … Oooh! G'bye!

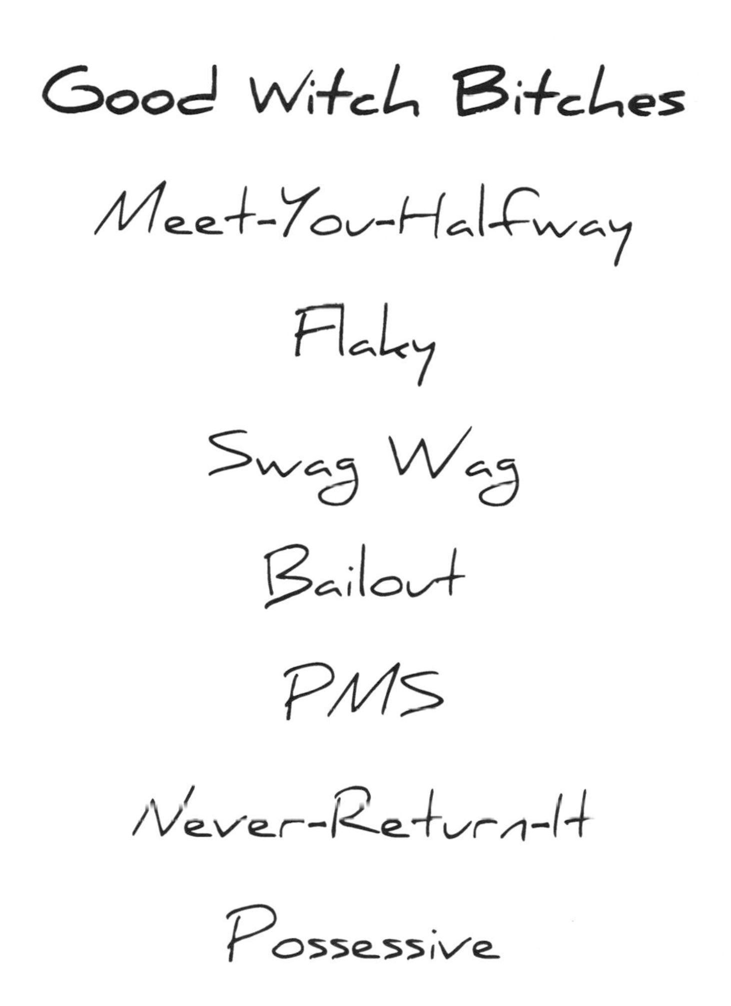
Good Witch Bitches
Meet-You-Halfway
Flaky
Swag Wag
Bailout
PMS
Never-Return-It
Possessive

Meet-You-Halfway

This type of bitch is extremely common, and such characteristics are embedded in people all over the world. In general, these bitches make decent friends. They differ from the Player Hater in that they truly like you. Feelings of jealousy can erupt at times, as is human nature, but they're not out to run you over like a Mack Truck.

Meet-You-Halfway Bitches do exactly what their name implies—they meet you halfway. They'll listen to your stories, problems, or gossip … but never for too long. They're ready and eager to spit out what's on their minds, and though they listen, it's usually with a somewhat deafened ears.

They'll join you for dinner if you pick them up, and it's highly unlikely they'll pick you up. If they do, then they get to choose what movie to see, which nightclub to dance at, or where to dine. Friendship is a game of give and take, but since you're probably not the only friend they're like this with, in their minds, their half-ass behavior is nothing out of the ordinary.

The basic step in handling a Meet-You-Halfway is realizing the person doesn't mean any harm by his or her way of thinking. While these bitches get the gist of your heartache, it's more important that you get theirs. During conversation, they'll usually let you speak first—that way, they can talk as long as they want when you're done. It's not that this type of bitch doesn't care that your car broke down, but this person wants your pity when it comes to the hole in the muffler of his or her car.

Another point about these bitches is that they're often overly dramatic about their problems. In fact, their problems may not even be that severe, but they sure make them sound as if they are—and often as if yours are nowhere near as bad as theirs are. Problems, problems, problems. It's a laundry list for the Meet-You-Halfway, and that's why they become bitchy at times. Sometimes they're so damn negative that you feel compelled to bitch too! They may drag you into their gutters, and before you know it, you're drudging up negative aspects of your life. Due to overanalyzing, you'll become convinced either that you have negativity in your life or you'll declare things negative just to make the bitch feel better. I warn you: don't become negative by default!

In general, it's wise to keep your triumphs to yourself when dealing with them. People who carry a negative attitude and live in complete "Me, Me, Me" worlds seldom acknowledge the "You, You, You" world. It's quite all right for you to have an "It's all about me" attitude, but there should also be a sincere amount of respect and compassion for others. Without other people, you wouldn't be able to flourish completely. Understand right now that to be at your best, it can't be about you all the time. Please don't get it twisted and don't get it confused.

In respect to the previous paragraph, understand that there will always be those who won't get it. Meet-You-Halfways are the perfect example. Because of this, you have to be careful when sharing private information with them. Remember that they only meet you halfway, so the point at which they can turn on you comes sooner than a real friend's would. You'll know you're dealing with Meet-You-Halfways if you question whether telling them trusted information was a wise choice.

In addition, think twice before telling them about any opportunities you're presented. Because these bitches often have negative perceptions of their own lives, they despise it when something is positive in yours. As a human being, you should strive for the better good of humanity; however, it shouldn't be in your nature to boast about your achievements, as doing so will certainly bring about hatred. Despite how humble you are, you must still use caution when telling anyone, especially these bitches, about your triumphs. You see, sometimes we trust people so much that we don't think they're capable of hate. Even if their lives aren't up to par, we don't want to believe they could be capable of envy.

I firmly believe that if you accumulate enough negative wishing and you're unprepared, it can thwart goals you have set for yourself. Say enough about an opportunity (whether it be creatively, professionally, or relationship related) to the wrong people and you can accrue enough hate to throw your situation in retrograde. I will touch on this subject later in the book, but for now remember to be selective with whom you share any life highlights.

Because it's possible that you've become doubtful, allow me to enlighten you. When you're overcome with excitement and joy about an opportunity, you may want to tell everyone you love the good news. I guarantee this already happened to some of you in the past—you told several people good news about an opportunity and in the end, the opportunity fell through. Then everyone asked, "What happened?" Some people may genuinely be interested and only ask once or twice, while others may ask repeatedly just to rub it in your face. Before you know it, you're sick of explaining, no matter who's asking. It's not unlikely that you'll have repeat offenders, as there could be people who bring up the issue over and over again, even after you've buried it.

It's almost as if the people who really care know when to back off and let the issue alone, while those who have even a twinge of jealousy will rehash the issue repeatedly just to hear you confirm that it didn't work in your favor. These people may act as if they care and pretend to show sympathy, but the truth is, your loss is music to their ears.

Meet-You-Halfway Bitches may convince themselves that they care, but inside, sometimes they can't ignore the deep-down chuckle they experience when you reiterate the details of loss. The tricky thing about Meet-You-Halfways is that they don't necessarily want to compete with you, yet they find themselves doing it. Meet-You-Halfway Bitches are transcendable because competing with you isn't their hearts' *true* desire. If anything, they become more starved for attention and are increasingly uncaring about your troubles. In their minds, nothing's worse than their troubles (and they're happy to explain why!). These bitches may have good hearts, but they're a little lost when it comes to the virtues of compassion and empathy.

They're often so overwhelmed with their problems that when decisions are made, things have to go their way. If not, then tantrums erupt. Remember the pity issue here: "Poor Me, Me, Me—I love you and all, but please say yes to Olive Garden. I've had a hell of a day, and I need a breadstick!"

You could smirk and say, "I don't speak 'Whinese,'" but if you truly want immediate results, simply tell it like it is. Moreover, because of their craving for attention, they'll become absorbed by the fact that you're speaking to them about them and not yourself. You don't have to be bitchy, but be honest. Point out to them that maybe their problems are a result of their own actions. Further, you can ask them to please reconsider what things in their lives are truly a problem and what aren't. Don't they ever stop to smell the roses? And if things are so bad, why not take a stance and fix them?

In my experience, less than half the time, they'll stop and truly consider what you're saying. The bad news, as I said before, is that Meet-You-Halfways don't get it. The good news is that they *can* get it. You can also expect plenty of whining to take place. Make sure you consistently address these bitches—"Karen, Karen, listen"—so it registers that they're still receiving attention. If you have to, pat them on their backs. Then clarify the situations and how they can be mended should they desire.

If they continue to be aggressive or bitchy with you, then let your Inner Bitch handle it. The next time they go berserk and start the bitchy attitude thing, go directly to the source of the problem and say, "Look, I know you're upset about XYZ, but don't take it out on me! I'm here to listen, not to absorb your negative energy." They may retort, "I'm not taking it out on you!" Don't turn this into a "Yes, you are/are not" game of idiocy. Just repeat the following: "I'm offering to listen. I'm *not* going to argue." Once they've agreed to not blow up and run in the other direction, you'll have your chance to communicate. Again, tell them about your thoughts and their situations. Lay it down! If they can't respect you at this point, then they're not Meet-You-Halfway Bitches, they're Total Bitches!

Again, Meet-You-Halfways don't necessarily want to compete with you, yet they find themselves doing it. If their attitudes are miserable, they'll certainly love some company. Don't settle! They *do* want your friendship, and they *do* like you (for the most part), but every now and then, they overindulge and swallow a large gulp of "hater-ade." In the long run, however, they'll value you and won't want to lose you. Just be patient, keep your Inner Bitch on guard, and wait with an open mind. If you give it time and don't force it, then maybe, just maybe, Meet-You-Halfways will go the total distance.

Flaky

Of all the chapters in this book, this one certainly hits home for most people. It had been tugging me at my leg for some time, and the more I experienced flakiness, the more compelled I was to write about it. Due to some type of cranium psychosis, we as a society not only rely on others for support, advice, and bonding, but we also depend heavily on others to fulfill some twisted voids within ourselves. In modern times, the term *flake* doesn't apply solely to the frosted corn cereal we have come to love so dearly. The term *flaky* has come to define anyone who untimely bails out of a commitment. These bitches may let you know with just enough time in advance, but the worst-case scenario is when they bail out without any heads-up. It's like giving an RSVP and then pulling a disappearing act. The problem is, there's only one person allowed to do that, and that's David Copperfield.

Since the flake is a multifaceted entity, there are many sides to examine and reflect on before you proceed in dealing with them. When the bitch at hand is a flake, then we should examine the person facet by facet. The first thing we should note is that in order for him or her to make flake status, the bitch must have committed to and canceled more than one consecutive appointment.

In order for these appointments to fully count, one of the following criteria must be met:

- The bitch called the day before or the day of to reschedule.
- The bitch called the day before or the day of to cancel (a reschedule pending).
- The bitch failed to show up with no call or effort to contact.

If any of the above occurs even once, it's a red flag that this person could be a flake. But since the Flaky Bitch has so many different levels, let's examine the circumstances further.

Your ego may be soothed when these bitches express a desire to reschedule. If that's truly the case, and it very well might be, then fantastic. However, please be aware that flakes may be saying this to take the heat off themselves. It's difficult for them to actually call you and tell you straight up that they can't make it, which is why they don't. If they contact you in time, they'll reschedule, but if they can't bring themselves to do even that, then they do nothing and decide to deal with it later.

No matter what the outcome of the broken commitment, take it as a sign that perhaps this person isn't what you hoped him or her to be. If these bitches consistently back out of plans with you, you should ask whether or not they even want anything to do with you. In most cases, they do. They just don't see you as a priority. If you really don't mean shit to them, then you probably won't get any further than a few unanswered calls (at which point you should give up—walk away with dignity!). If you keep making plans with someone and shit consistently comes up, causing the person to reschedule, then it's your job to stand back and say, "You know what? You're obviously very busy. Call me when you're ready." This leaves the door open to these bitches while also letting them know you're no longer relying on them for solid plans.

This type of situation can be extremely annoying, especially if you're in that odd stage where you'd like to get to know these people better but you have certain barriers to break down. This is a tricky issue—at this point, you're forced to differentiate between those who are genuinely busy and those who are too afraid to shut you down.

If you reflect on all your relationships, it doesn't matter who was more persistent in the beginning. At some point, someone reached out and the other accepted the offer, allowing a connection to be made. For some relations, this occurrence could've happened in a snap. For others, it could've taken months, years, even decades! Does the time it took dictate whether the relationship was meaningful or worthwhile? Most certainly not! Patience is one of the greatest virtues we can possess. I know we all want what we want when we want it … in the exact way we say we want it. But since that rarely happens, what's the next best alternative?

How about this: We get what we want the way we want it, just not when we want it. The only thing that changes in this equation is time. It's better to give it some time instead of hurrying the fuck up and ending up with a less-than-perfect result, right? And when it comes to the Flaky Bitches, time is the culprit. If you make plans to get together at a certain time and these people don't hold up their ends of the bargain, then they're flakes, right? Right. Therefore, they should be denounced and badgered until they go cross-eyed, right? *Wrong!*

This is where we really get into the depths of the flakes' psyches. It is unacceptable, no matter what, to make plans with someone and not show up. I don't care if you lost your cell phone (there's such thing as a pay phone), if you were in the ER all night (where there are phones), if your car got towed (you can still access a phone), or if you got held up late at work (where there's a phone.) If your dog or kid is sick, if you got pulled over, or if you're so damn broke that both your cell and house service have been shut off, there are still pay phones.

Blame it on Sprint or AT&T, but the bottom line is that phones exist on every dimension, plane, and metaphysical state in the universe—well, for the most part. The only way a phone call is not possible is if you're dead. Other than that, if there's no phone call, only one thing is a fact: it's a shyster's move and Total Bitch behavior. That's all you need to know.

Handling the Flaky Bitch boils down to how much you really want the person in your life. The answer to this question may vary depending on how this person went about flaking. If he or she didn't straight up call, notify you, or offer an explanation, then I'd seriously reconsider the bitch's manners and morale. If the person cancelled and rescheduled, then you should probably give him or her the benefit of the doubt.

Obviously, you want to get to know this person; otherwise, there wouldn't have been an engagement to begin with. If you're the recipient of the flakiness and not the one being flaky, then realize that others sometimes need persistence from interested parties. When it comes to keeping a connection alive, if you really think this person is worth something, then be aware that the resistance could stem from something other than you. It's possible this person has experienced many flakes as well, or perhaps circumstances really did change.

The key is to know the difference between someone who needs a little nudge and one who needs a first-class ticket out of your life. It's admirable when one person takes an initiative to plant the seed of a beautiful relationship. At best, the seed blossoms into a flower of friendship, compassion, and unconditional love. However, you can't push too hard or you run the risk of driving the person away completely. If you take persistence to an unnecessary level, you may appear desperate, psychotic, or obsessed with the other party.

If people are consistently flaky, you must consider why you like them. Do you *really* like them, or is there another reason you want to keep the connection? Be as honest with yourself as possible, as this is the only way you'll be able to understand your concerns and cares about them. At times, it may be hard to face rejection, so we persist in an effort to make a person connect with us. Don't bother—leave your ego behind and move on. Forcing a relationship, or any connection for that matter, will only put pressure on the person as well as yourself. Friendships aren't created through pressure; they're created from a mutual flow of respect, curiosity, and genuine interest in one another.

Flakiness parallels cowardliness, but in the trials of life, even the coward is entitled to some defense. I know we don't like to acknowledge or even fathom the thought of life existing outside of ourselves. This fact can be brutal and it might suck, but the bottom line is that every soul on this earth has something called a *life*. Sometimes you're factored into someone's equation, and other times you're not factored in at all.

We can all be flaky at times, and I am not one to play innocent. Have I been one before? Absolutely! There have been times when I knew damn well I was supposed to be somewhere, that I was supposed to place a phone call, or that I was supposed to drive someone to the airport. Did I follow through? No, I wasn't able to. Was that flaky of me? Yes. Was it right? No. I don't liking flaking on people, and I try my hardest to be a woman of my word. But my life, as well as yours, wasn't created to constantly cater to other people consistently. Furthermore, we weren't created to consistently rescue others. I love meeting and helping people; I'm a Sagittarius, for Pete's sake, so I really don't have a choice. Yet despite this trait, I also need *me* time. Well, guess what. So does everyone else on the planet! (Some people, like our president, shouldn't give a flying fuck about *me* time. He should be consumed by *our* time.)

There's no denying that being a flake act is wrong. I'm certain either I've paid off my karma or I still have it coming, but that's hardly the focus. The focus, my dear reader, is yourself. Aside from being honest with yourself and recalling the times when you were a total flake monster, take a moment to rationalize further and connect with your Inner Bitch.

When you've flaked in the past, why did you display such behavior? I think that you'll find that many times you avoided an official cancellation because you were fearful of the other person's reaction. It can be quite a predicament when someone has cornered you into an engagement that isn't your cup of tea. You listened to some spiel, couldn't quite say no, and before you could scream "Corn Flakes!" you were booby-trapped into some seminar, dinner party, or at the very worst, a date. Think about it: You're sitting at home on the couch, twiddling your thumbs with a repetitive mantra: "Don't go! Don't go! You're only going in order to please the crowd."

With all your soul, you truly don't wanna go. However, the anxiety of calling and canceling is so unbearable that you go against your own wishes and show up. Maybe you'll have a great time—that's what we all hope for. But maybe, out of angst, you'll end up downing a shitload of nachos and go home more irritated with yourself than ever.

If you do decide to tough it out, then tough it out until the end! If you show up to, say, a birthday party where the Chex Mix could be Kibbles 'n Bits, then remember that *you* made the decision to show up so *you* play the part! Don't fight with yourself and go just because you're too pansy to call, but if you do, don't you dare bitch!

There are a few reasons why one would flake. One is that this person could simply be a loner. A loner (and I define this loosely) is someone who can hang with the highs, the lows, and everything in between. What's more, that person can take you or leave you. There really is no leaving a loner, for before you've made up your mind, it's possible that person is gone and doesn't give a shit.

But with true flaky people, you have to put your ego aside and honestly consider the situation. You see, most people that are deemed "flaky" really aren't at all. These people could be very busy (remember what I said about having a life?). Their schedules may change day to day due to a job, their families, spouses-to-be, or newborn Chihuahuas that shit everywhere. Who's really to know? No one, including you, so you have to take what is said as the truth. If this person keeps up the no-show attitude, then ask yourself:

1) Who's really pursuing this meeting?
2) How many times has this person cancelled?
3) To what degree of severity was the flake offense?

4) Did I get advance notice or was it a last-minute thing?
5) Why do I give a fuck?

Flakes often won't see their lack of consideration as a faux pas. They regard themselves as people of high esteem and righteousness, and their not making your date wasn't because they don't like you but because other conditions demanded their time.

With many Flaky Bitches, the thought that you might be insulted never enters their minds. They literally have so much shit in their faces that even Chanel ski goggles can't shield them, so what do they do? They cancel—consistently. Don't take it personally. It's highly unlikely that you're the only one who is a victim to them.

These bitches sound self-centered, but not all of them are. They leap throughout life like Brazilian tree frogs (but the Brazilian tree frog doesn't have appointment after appointment).

Flaky doesn't always mean bitch either. Busy, perhaps. More than that, too busy to deal with someone else's attitude! Just imagine if, after making the conscious decision to cancel a meeting, you were bombarded with (feel free to say the following aloud in a whiney voice):

- "Why can't you come?"
- "But you said you would!"

- "How can you say yes and then no?"
- "I'm counting on you!"
- "You flake!"

Hold it right there, partner. What if someone were badgering *you* on and on? No wonder we let our cell phones keep ringing and home answering machines pick up! If people think you're going to be overly defensive, they'll avoid you. Only God may know, but even He's over it! *It's too much drama, too much*! It's essential to realize that people will resist manipulative and overbearing souls when they can. Give them their space and they'll want you to occupy it.

Over the years, I have concluded that the term "flake" is tossed around like a football. Many people have been deemed flakes when, in fact, quite the contrary was true. Because I've been called a flake when completely inapplicable, I grow irritated when this term is abused. When I flake, you don't have to call me on it, as I already know. Other certain instances had nothing to do with my being flaky. Indeed, 99 percent of the time, it was due to my being too damn busy to do whatever I was "flaking" on. At first, I took it personally when people called me a flake, but then I started to realize they were simply expecting much more of me than I could agree to. After a while, I stopped making agreements or arrangements.

I'm not a notorious flake, but I will say this: there are times, trials, and personal agendas that have to be handled. I've said it twice, and I'll say it again: there is something called *life*.

Coinciding with you in that fabulous all-encompassing spectrum of particles, time, and light are tasks and mandatory obligations. It's so much easier sometimes not to call just to avoid being hassled. No one wants to be nagged, so why call? There's truly no incentive. I know we all want to believe that we're the ultimate incentive. If you and your clone were the only two people left in the galaxy, I'm sure you wouldn't flake on each other. That's fantastic, fabulous, and frickin' awesome! But those circumstances are highly bloody unlikely. Thus you must deal with the rest of the population.

Once again, it stems from the root from which you are planted. If you feel this person is genuine and sincere, then don't immediately give up! If someone is a busy little bee, then you absolutely must respect that person. There's a difference between someone who flakes for bona fide reasons and one who simply can't commit.

Be honest, no matter what your motives are. I've found that if you have a serious one-on-one with yourself, you can alleviate a lot of uncertainty and heal a bruised ego. Usually when people reject you, it's because you're trying too hard. Trying too hard means you've gone over the edge and are being obvious. If such is the case, you really have to get in touch with yourself. Once you ask and answer the questions posed earlier, you can better evaluate whether you truly want this person in your life. What's more, you can figure out why he or she has such a grasp on you.

Often with human nature, when we're told something is off limits, we want it even more. Do we *really* want it or need it? Nah—we just want to prove we can get it, use it, and discard it. As humans, we honestly don't give resistance a lot of consideration. Our egos supersede us, causing us to think, *It doesn't matter if my actions cause a negative effect; I just want to prove I can have it!*

That voice of retaliation and resistance has one small name, my friends. As small a name as it is, it's one hell of a concept. More than anything, its power is so vivid and real that it often suppresses efforts to establish balance. The word is *ego.* Unfortunately, we're each born with one, which is why it can hurt so much to let someone flake the fuck off. I ask you to see it for what it is. With a little honesty and thoughtful consideration, you'll better be able to assess whether this person is worth your time.

Trust your gut instincts and avoid being flaky on your part. If you do your part, you'll always be confident about who you are and what you represent. As for everyone else, it's completely up to you whether you pursue any connection or leave their Frosted Flaky asses for the grocery store shelf.

Swag Wag

These particular bitches only hang around you when there is something in it for them, and I don't mean just emotionally. These bitches capitalize on your hard work, your monetary well-being, and are as cheap as dirt. Dirt is pretty damn cheap. You usually hang out with these people as a last resort, and they usually behave the way they do because they get accustomed to your compliant attitude. In reality, it boils down to the difference between their income and your income. More than likely, if you are an above average to wealthy person, you have been a victim of the Swag-Wag Bitch. These bitches think you're rich even when they're completely off target.

I have always been one to enjoy nice things: labels, logos, and fine fabrics. What can I say? I am a material girl in a material world, and I don't sleep on any sheets with less than an eight hundred thread count. I can't help the fact that when I was only an eleven-year-old fledgling, I could slam open an issue of *Vogue*, close my eyes and point, and still land on something Chanel. My blessings of fortune have adorned me (at times) with fine things in life, and because of this I have grown to be very generous—so generous that at times people cross the friendship line of accepting, turning it into milking. They love the idea of fine swag!

I've had a couple of friends, one in particular, who turned into a total Swag Wag Bitch. What I mean by that is that no matter where we went or how much we spent, I took up the tab. I'm a very easygoing person, but my Inner Bitch should have been stronger. After hundred-dollar-plus (but mostly in the fifty-sixty dollar range) checks, you would *think* she would offer to pay something. At the very least, you'd think she'd chip in or demand to leave a tip. I was raised to always pay my own way, and no matter what, I always offer to.

Offering, whether or not you can afford it, shows character and humility. It's about sacrifice. I don't care if you're dining with Bill Gates and you have one buck left to your name—offer it anyway because you are showing that this person is meaningful enough for you to spend a bill or two. With the particular bitch I experienced, I never asked for half or any type of payment. Asking for payment in itself lacks class. You shouldn't have to say a word; the offer should be out there immediately. It's not as if you agreed to go to dinner with this bitch without the person knowing that ta-da—dinner costs money! If you add liquor, you've got extra weight on the bill.

My Inner Bitch should've called out at times, and I openly admit that I let it get out of hand with some. No, it's like that. If can afford to go to nice places for brunch and I enjoy their company, I'll take care of the bill. Still, they should be genuine enough to either decline and suggest somewhere else if they can't afford it. But at my insistence of the Ritz Carlton over Denny's, they should accept me as a nice person, as someone who doesn't care about how much they can afford or if they can pay me back. I don't like to put people on the spot, and I don't like to make others feel as if we have to go to the Four Seasons if all they can afford is IHOP.

I love IHOP (I love their cheese grits and their Rooty Tooty Fresh N' Fruitys.) We can even cook at home (just bust out the grill). The bottom line? I just want your friendship. But as much as I value friendships, there are times when I like to treat others to something super-extraordinary. It gives me great pleasure, and if you're someone I care about, you bet your britches I'll whip up something extra special.

I love life, I enjoy great dinners, and if I enjoy someone's company, I want that person to enjoy dinner too. Here and there, it's fine. It's not as if I expect you to treat everyone to everything all the time. But even if you did, for argument's sake, lavish good fortune among your friends, they at least need to reciprocate by being tried-and-true. They should truly value and appreciate you for your never asking for reciprocation. If they have a problem reciprocating, in any way, shape, or form, then they should *not* accept the invitation.

I used to make the mistake of thinking that if I treated the less fortunate (and I am speaking only in the context of this one bitch experience; I am not saying everyone I have dined with is less fortunate by any means), not only could we enjoy a shared moment of luxury, but that this person would also hold me in high regard because of my generosity. My intentions were to perform a selfless act that showed that, despite the cost, if the person truly couldn't afford it, I would pay his or her way only in exchange for the companionship. But buyer beware! There's no such thing as a free lunch, and these friends can disappear quickly, along with your bank account.

After about two or three instances with these bitches, I know that you get a moocher now and again. I was recently dining with a new buddy for the first time alone, and we went to my favorite restaurant, T.G.I. Friday's. This was the first time I had dined alone with this guy. When the bill came, I automatically grabbed it and said, "My treat, please." I meant it. I wanted to. I enjoyed this person, and even though he could very easily pay his portion, I really wanted to treat. But this person—my dear, sweet, adorable, and drop-dead gorgeous friend Josh—replied, "No." Firmly but politely.

I may have hesitated; I don't really remember. But what does ring familiar is the "no." It was so refreshing because he could have easily accepted and abused the offer. You can use this tactic to gauge someone's sincerity. It's bad on your part to cater to or encourage this trait. If you have treated more than once and there is no attempt to reciprocate, then you have already opened the floodgates for abuse. No reciprocation on someone else's part is Total Bitch behavior. But please have hope in knowing that karma will take care of these bitches. Still, don't have too much faith that karma will take care of them and don't give too much of yourself so that you have to depend on karma to do all the magic work.

Bailout

This is a bitch who, for whatever reason, ups and leaves while you're hanging with him or her. The sudden act of bailing can happen anywhere, but it's most annoying while out partying with someone, when you're halfway into your date, or that person is your ride home! These bitches differ from Flaky Bitches in that they actually show up, but they bail out unexpectedly and do it with bad timing.

If you're having a great time with someone, you want to extend the pleasure. Likewise, if you're counting on hanging with this person all day or night (or both), it can be gut-wrenching to have him or her suddenly swoop up the keys and dip out. Something unforeseen triggers this fight-or-flight reaction, and though no doubt alarming, it's downright disappointing when someone wigs out and goes home! This behavior is rude. If someone pulls this stunt, he or she is being selfish.

If these bitches in question have been tried-and-true troopers in the past, they deserve a little break here and there. They'd better be workhorses for the friendship, although I don't know how real friends could bail out on you. That's something to think about. If friends leave you suddenly and you were clearly expecting more of them, then start paying attention because they could have a habit. If they're repeat offenders, I'd question their loyalty. Unless someone has a board meeting with the president of the United States the next morning, there is no excuse to unexpectedly announce that he or she is bailing out. If someone has the next day to chill and the biggest task is getting the oil changed, then it's only good etiquette to stay. I don't care who you are. You owe it to your friends to hang tough. To bail out is selfish, wrong, and unethical.

You'll often find that the reason this person bails out is because he or she is thinking of someone else. Who might that person be? It varies from Bailout Bitch to Bailout Bitch, but whoever the person is, he or she *is more important than you are*. It could be someone's mother, someone's lover, someone's love interest, another friend … or more than one person. It's likely that for whatever reason, this particular person scares the Bailout Bitch. He or she fears that person and always has him or her tucked in the back of the mind. Then, when the bitch has been somewhere too long or it gets to be the wee hours of the morning, the person packs his or her shit and splits. What sucks about these bitches in particular is that they're usually cool people, which is why you're so hurt when they leave you. As cool as they are, they have an injected fear of what someone else will think if they don't report to home or sleep in their own beds.

Handling a Bailout Bitch is a matter of preplanning. If, for instance, you plan to party with this person and don't want to go home alone, you can opt to pack your stuff and stay at his or her place. Partying at your place is an open invitation for someone to bail on you. You may also take the verbal route and speak up—just bust it out. With intent, lock eyes with the bitch and say, "Look, I adore the shit out of you, but if we're gonna hang, we're gonna hang. I need this from you before we go out all night [or go to the opera, take a weekend vacation, or what have you]."

Remember, these bitches are heavily influenced by what someone else thinks. They're pleasers and try to mold themselves into what others want them to be. You can try to intimidate them into what you want them to be (a friend who stays put), but I find this train of thought somewhat mindless. Your goal isn't to intimidate anyone; it's to earn respect, compassion, and trust.

Unfortunately, with this type of bitch, the bailing out may occur here and there until you ultimately form the strongest of bonds. Be certain that you're not the one being selfish if the reason is a true emergency or something you'd bail out for, and pay attention if the bitch implies that he or she fears someone else. Always bear in mind the fear factor of "*they*". Somehow, no matter how small, "*they*" hold a piece of these bitches prisoner. You never want to become one of "*them*" so be patient despite your disappointments. The day they no longer bail, it means they avoided jail. Because you are a good friend, let the bitch know that he or she can stay around with no penalty!

PMS

No, PMS doesn't stand for "putting up with men's shit." Rather, it's a phenomenon that happens to many women every month for quite some time during their life spans. It can be a terror indeed, but understanding the characteristics of a PMS Bitch versus some other type of bitch is crucial in maintaining relationships.

It's hard for some people, especially men, to fathom that PMS can be so intense for a woman that she will suddenly trade her car for a broomstick. The bad news is that it's possible. The good news is that it's manageable. Anyone who is dealing with mood swings, crying spells, and tension all at the same time is absolutely running the risk of turning into the Wicked Witch of the West. What's more, physical symptoms like acne, weight gain, and constipation can make for a very sad state of mind as your body is going into psycho mode. So psycho that one feels as if she is psycho—and you believe it too! Introducing the PMS Bitch.

You will realize you're dealing with a PMS Bitch when one minute she's as sweet as cupcake frosting (yum!) and the next minute she's a total rotten apple with a green worm slithering out of it. And those who set her off risk being grabbed by the hair and getting their heads ripped off. Then the PMS Bitch swings the head around like one of those medieval ball and chains and bludgeons what's left of the body with it.

Then she retreats and cries over what she's done, but then she's suddenly tired from all the crying. So she takes a nap or goes into a deep sleep, and when she wakes, she's happy again.

Yup, that's pretty much how it goes. Well, something like that. Another symptom is poor concentration, so she might actually rip your head off but miss her mark on your body. Yup, something like that.

That's just the mental aspect; there's a physical aspect too. In essence, the bitch feels like crap, but she can't take a crap because all her crap is backed up in her stomach bloat. All the toxins built up along with whatever garbage she ate (as cravings run rampant), which causes acne, further frustrates the situation.

It's hard to deal with PMS Bitches because while it's temporary, it can range from complete rage in a woman to a more somber state, and she wouldn't normally behave that way. So having sympathy is key. Knowing that the woman you are dealing with is suffering (which is why they call it *suffering* from PMS), taking certain measures to reduce the symptoms is crucial.

Approaching the bitch can be like dealing with a huge growling dog. Never try for a showdown, as the dog will bite. As mean and evil as the bitch may seem, don't retaliate. Even if she says terrible things to you, realize you are dealing with someone else, so don't exacerbate the situation by telling her to pull the tampon out of her ass. Don't take it personally! You have to approach it as if meeting a dog for the first time. Hold out your hand and let her know you have good intentions. Let her smell your hand if necessary.

If the bitch is showing physical signs such as acne and bloating, suggest going to a holistic store or health food store and buying a cleanse. This will help in the process of elimination, which will reduce the bloating and the acne by ridding the toxic buildup. Moreover, for salt and water retention, potassium magnesium supplements will help, as will dandelion root. You can also suggest dandelion tea (if she's into tea) or St. John's Wort Blues Away tea.

Chamomile? Very good for mood swings. So is exercise—even a brisk walk will kick in those endorphins. Day spas are great if they have a sauna, as sweating will definitely help with the salt retention, and sweating in general is a wonder for feeling lighter and overall happier. For a good night's rest, lavender on a pillow and three milligrams of melatonin will ease any cramping or irritability that may keep the bitch awake. In reality, PMS Bitches are in need of support and help. But by managing it correctly, symptoms can be eased to where you can keep your head on long enough to make these suggestions.

Obviously, if the PMS Bitch doesn't want help and bites your hand, simply walk away! Some women need alone time because other things that may be bothering them are magnified at this fragile time of the month. So if you feel it's more bite than bark, bow out gracefully and then call her when you're PMSing and bite her back! Juuuust kidding. Just walk away and within two weeks, when all is said and done, the "real" person will come back and you can resume your relationship until the next month, when she goes bitch again.

Never-Return-It

When I was in college, I came across a Never-Return-It Bitch that also displayed some psycho tendencies. In the end, I was forced to call the police on her because she wouldn't return one of my beloved outfits that I'd left at her home. I was moving from my college town to New York City, and I feared I'd never see my outfit again.

When I tried to collect the garments, a one-of-a kind hand-painted brown top with a denim skirt and cream leather boots, she wouldn't answer or return my calls. I went by her work, but it turned out she had quit her job, making it even more difficult to get hold of her. I even returned to the apartment where I had left the clothes and learned she had moved. The office had no written record where she had relocated, and the day I went there, the computers were down, making it impossible for even the landlords to contact her!

I had proof the outfit was mine because the last time I had worn it was on her birthday. We went out with a group of people and took several pictures, which clearly showed me wearing it. I moved to New York City empty-handed, but never once did I forget the outfit I held so dear. Not only was it badass, but it was also new. My mother had dropped mad stacks on it for a television show, and I was devastated.

Even after I moved, I kept calling her cell phone. Through the works of serendipity, it turned out that my friend Michelle (still in college) used to be good friends with this girl back in the day and gave me her parents' phone number. I immediately called them and asked for her new home number. Her father (the SOB) wouldn't budge and told me she would call me if she wanted to! He wasn't aware of the situation, but I could tell by the tone of his voice that he was a stingy person.

My mother even called her, pleading for the safe return of the items, as did my best friend.

Finally, after a couple months of silly games, I called the police. I explained the situation and asked for some type of intervention! I simply wouldn't stand for such unfairness. I don't think I have ever borrowed anything from anyone without returning it. The next day as I left acting school, I checked my cell phone, only to find several missed calls (all marked urgent). After all those months, she had finally called. I went inside a bathroom at Kinko's on Lexington Avenue so I could hear the messages clearly. I dialed her number. The phone began to ring, and there was no chance for a second ring before I was greeted by a high-pitched shriek: "What the *hell* do you think you're doing calling the police on me! They called me today and said that if I didn't hand over your clothes, I'd be arrested! I can't believe you're this psycho about your clothes!" Then the signal faded.

My Inner Bitch began to grow horns. I couldn't contain myself in the small restroom, so I stepped back onto the street and called back. It was obvious I wouldn't have trouble hearing her.

The phone started ringing. I began tapping my foot on the pavement, lips pursed. My eyes perused the buildings around me, my right ear taking in honking taxi horns and my left waiting for an answer.

She answered with a stern hello, and I explained to her ever so politely that I was not psycho about my clothes. The problem was that the outfit was not only expensive but also very dear to me. We were talking about a grand worth of clothing, and I already had three pairs of Chanel shoes stolen from me, as well as a pair of glasses and a necklace.

She yelled, she screamed, she bitched. She hung up the phone and called back, then hung up on me again. Then I called back. I hadn't really gotten into it like that with someone in a while—it had been at least two good two years. We even threw around some legal threats, which really added to the flavor and intensity of the battle. The bitch had gotten me at the wrong point in my life—it wasn't gonna go her way. That very next morning, she handed over my precious items to my best friend, and within a week, I was reunited with my belongings.

There have probably been times when you've lent things out, only to never have them returned. It sucks, which is why I hate lending shit. I do, but I shouldn't. These bitches come in three forms:

1) Those you lend stuff to and they break it or ruin it
2) Those you lend stuff to and they forget to return it
3) Those you lend stuff to and they lose it

Sometimes you don't even lend it; you just leave it behind on accident and trust that you can reclaim what's yours within a matter of days. I have left shoes at two separate homes, only to learn they had been "lost." When I asked one of the bitches if I could come by and pick up my shoes, she said she wasn't sure where they were. I had left them right there in plain view under the coffee table, but she didn't recall seeing a pair of gold Chanel shoes anywhere. She did say that maybe she'd swept them into the closet—where she clearly swept things that weren't hers. I never saw those shoes again.

Word from the wise: don't ever lend your stuff if you can't afford to see it go. Make that the number one rule. Rule number two? If you do break rule one, set a return date and make sure the person has the money to replace it! At the very least, hold something for collateral. Rule number three is to stay on the person's ass, and if he or she fails to return or replace lost/damaged goods, then threaten to take legal action. Don't only threaten but actually consider it. There is such a thing called small claims court. Doing this will terminate your friendship, so it depends on the severity of the situation. The severity is based on what the bitch has of yours, the lack of willingness to comply, and beyond that, how much stuff you've had jacked in the past.

Possessive

Possessive Bitches are twofold. On the one hand, possessiveness in the forms of these bitches can often be looked at in a flattering light, hence they are Good Witch Bitches. On the other hand, there is a darker and more sinister type of a Possessive Bitch. Therefore, there are two types: those who want you just for themselves and see everyone else in your life as a threat and those who are possessive because they worry about you and don't want the wrong people to influence or harm you.

With the latter types of Possessive Bitches, can they be flattering? Perhaps. Annoying? Definitely. These bitches have to know that you have choices in life and that you can take care of yourself. This chapter examines the traits of Possessive Bitches and offers tactics to encourage their release of you, also showing you can use your Inner Bitch to take complete control and explode out of someone's supposed grasp on you.

You can have more than one Possessive Bitch at a time—in fact, you can have multiple. You can have, for instance, more than one who guards you like the Hope Diamond and more than one who wants to steal you like the Hope Diamond. I have had people working for me professionally who guarded me, where, at the same time, I had "friends" who wanted me every second and wanted to consume my time so that I couldn't produce or move forward. These bitches can be dangerous because when most people think of possessive, the first thing that comes to mind is a possessive lover. While that is definitely many times the case, being possessive takes on many forms and if at any time someone's possessiveness becomes detrimental to your health, well-being, or life, then you aren't dealing with a Possessive Bitch—you're dealing with a psychopath.

Knowing which is which is pretty obvious, but with the possessive types that guard, it can often feel overbearing because they don't trust anyone's intentions and you begin to feel like you've gained an extra parent. Just add milk. Sometimes you feel you can't make decisions for yourself with the guardian types because they are genuinely concerned and feel they know best. Often they convince you that they do, in fact. They have such a type of control that if you're hanging around someone that they don't feel is trustworthy or is a bitch, they may convince you this is the case—even if it isn't. It's possible that they're right, as sometimes four eyes are better than two, but you have to trust your instincts and know that if *you* suspect someone is up to no good, you can utilize your Inner Bitch to deal with that person.

This people become bitches when you retaliate against their thoughts or when they start to control who you hang around or where you go. Even though they have good intentions, this type of possessiveness can definitely get out of hand. These are the key characteristics of a guardian Possessive Bitch:

1) They start to take on role as mother or father figure in your eyes. They become annoyed, agitated, or upset if you don't listen to their "advice."
2) They don't trust many people around you, but others are in their good graces. They go out of their way to do nice gestures for you, even if you didn't ask them to.

What's interesting about this type of bitch is that they mirror a lot of how family and friends would normally behave. But again, when the boundaries cross from concern to control, it becomes really annoying and you have to handle it before it becomes out of control. Meanwhile, we have the sinister Possessive Bitch, who has a different type of grasp of you; this is highly manipulative. These bitches often display other types of bitch characteristics described in the book, such as the Player Hater. They can often show shades of the Sabotaging Bitch as well, but with the help of this book, you'll be able to determine if they are in fact showing more than one trait (thus making them Binary, Triple, or Super Bitches).

These types often make you feel insecure, physically and mentally, and are passive-aggressive in nature. So let's say you have a new dress you want to wear and it's a little shorter than what you usually wear. They may say, "Oh, that dress is very nice. But I thought you didn't want to show your legs until you completed all those private training sessions." Total Bitches. Now, while that's a bitchy thing to say, what does that have to do with possessiveness?

It has everything to do with it because these bitches are making you feel insecure and therefore controlling you. And control is what possessiveness is all about. Often the sinister Possessive Bitches will want to consume your time. They wear masks and want you morning, noon, and night. They call you often, even if you explain you don't have time. I had a "friend" who *literally* rang my phone every damn day for years, but there is a difference between someone calling and having a chat or calling a few times a day and actually *talking* versus someone who calls and you don't answer so they keep calling and calling and calling with no answer until you *do* answer. This is a major sign of possessiveness.

I know from personal experience that some Possessive Bitch have patterns. They will initially call and leave a message. Half an hour later, they will call again. Twenty minutes later, the phone will ring again. Fifteen minutes later, ten minutes later, five minutes later, and then every damn minute for about eight to ten minutes... It can be not only psychotic but also disturbing and annoying and cause the dissolution of a friendship.

Is it because these bitches really want you? No. It's because they are insecure themselves and become attached to you so that you can be just like them: insecure, with no time for advancement. This makes them feel better because it keeps you on their "level," and when someone else points this out, they become pissed off and try to pull the leash even tighter. What's more, they don't like anyone at all around you that may serve as an influence to see the bitches for who they are.

This is a major red flag. Moreover, they may pull the infamous "What about me!" card and whine and whine about how you don't pay as much attention to them as so-and-so; that you don't love them or care about them; blah, blah, blah. To recap, here are some key characteristics of the sinister Possessive Bitches:

1) They are time consuming in an effort to keep you from your life outside of them.
2) They don't like anyone you associate with.
3) They call often in ridiculous amounts of time intervals (often a pattern).
4) They play a guilt card on you to make you feel bad.
5) They are passive-aggressive or overly complimentary (extreme behavior).

Dealing with Possessive Bitches is hard because they can be one of two, obviously.

Communication is key, so you have to be firm with both types. For guardian possessives, I would recommend explaining to them that you can make your own decisions, that you are a responsible individual, that you appreciate they're looking out for you, but that in order to grow, you need to have autonomy in your life. These forms of bitches can be transcended with a good firm talking to. But behold and be bold!

If they continue with the behavior, then up the ante and tell them directly that they're risking your friendship by being so parenting. Lay it down! Tell them you don't need parenting and then point out something that you wish you could control about them. Think about what that would be in advance and have a few in your arsenal, just in case. But focus on one and turn the tables. Tell this person, "Well, I get really concerned when I see you with that bitch Joan who speaks so condescendingly to you." Or you could say, "I don't think letting your Chihuahua shit in the park without using a pooper scooper is appropriate." And mean it!

If you're doing something that you inherently know they are right about or engaging with people you know are not good to be around, then don't be a Dumb Bitch. But if the Possessive Bitch is getting on your last nerve over things that have no basis for advice, then you show that person how it feels to be parented and let it rip, honey.

Now, as far as the sinister types, I would start by telling them that you know what they're driving at with the passive-aggressive crap and that they won't win. Just by telling them that you know what those snide remarks really mean, you're essentially calling them out. This will signal to the bitches that you can't be manipulated because you're "a smart bitch, bitch." And they will back off.

If you have the types that call all the time, tell them that if they don't stop, you're going to block their calls via your phone service. Never admit it drives you crazy, as they may retaliate against your Inner Bitch by harassing more. Just keep it simple, and if they don't behave, then block them. It's usually free to block numbers for up to six months with any phone service including cell phones. If they're playing the guilt card, explain that they are the ones who should feel guilty because their jealousy and (keyword here) possessiveness are ruining your relationship. And you have a life, other friends, family, and a newborn Chihuahua that shits everywhere. If anything, the Chihuahua should have your full attention and time. Again, lay it down!

If the behavior continues, please get rid of these sinister bitches. They're so toxic and simply unwarranted and unneeded. Take control of your life and be possessive of yourself! Let your Inner Bitch be the one who controls what you do and who you associate with. With that mentality, you will never have a concern of being held down, for you will have broken from the Possessive Bitch bondage.

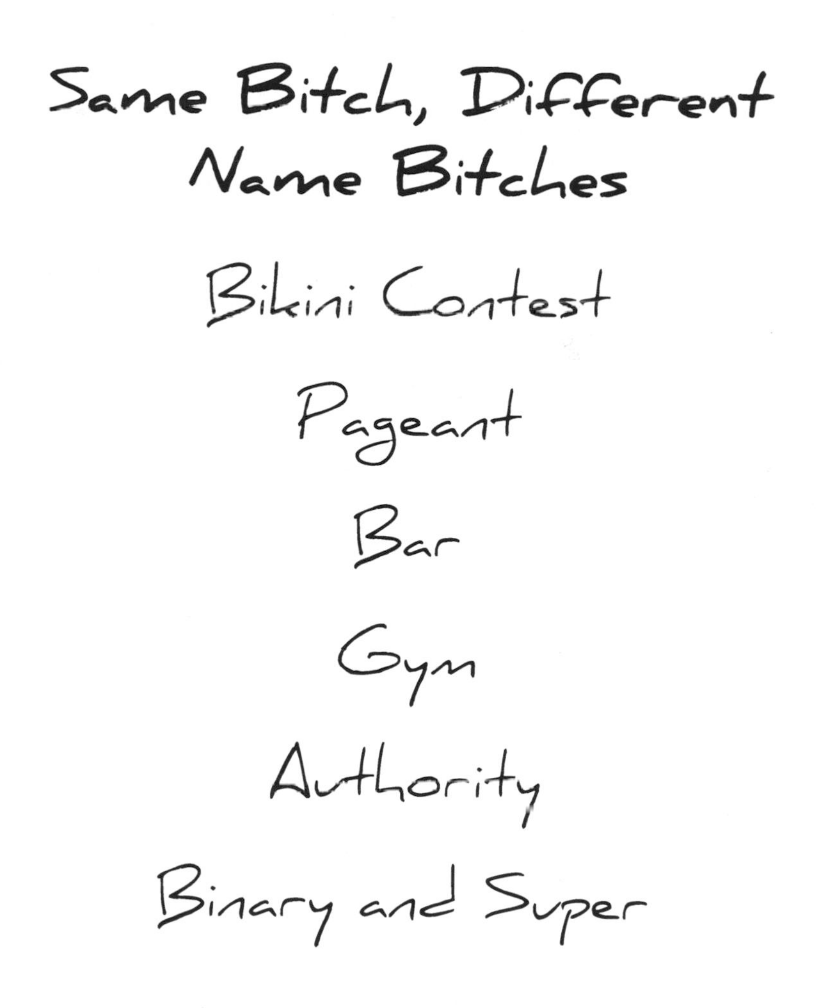
Same Bitch, Different Name Bitches
Bikini Contest
Pageant
Bar
Gym
Authority
Binary and Super

Bikini Contest

I know it seems that I have done it all. I have. I have even done bikini contests. The slut sister of all beauty pageants, bikini contests have been multiplying in large numbers since the mid-eighties. Women compete not so much for a title but for something tangible (such as money to pay the electric bill). A bikini contest winner usually takes home anywhere from two hundred to a thousand bucks, although I have competed in bikini competitions that had prizes of ten thousand dollars or more. Besides the obvious cash, other prizes have put a grin on my face: durable luggage sets, international trips, and quite a few professional tooth-whitening treatments. Talk about having two rows of Chiclets if you win!

But like bitches in the quest for a crown, Bikini Bitches also hold the thought of winning very dear to their hearts. It's an addiction, a double-edged-sword. You hate the contests when you lose, but you love them when you win. Possibly coming in first is dangled in your face like a carrot. To win five hundred dollars or more just for walking in front of people in a bikini doesn't seem so shameful to me. But if you lose, you basically walked in front of people in a bikini for free. It sucks when that happens, so you definitely go into it with a winning attitude.

Bikini bitches appear bitchier on the surface than the pageant ones. This is because bikini competitions don't last that long—a few hours at best—so there is no incentive to be crowned Miss Congeniality. I give pageant girls props on their ability to keep mum and control their tempers (the majority anyway.) But this ability doesn't make them any less bitchy than Bikini Bitches. In a sense, I give props to Bikini Bitches for being so up front because at least you know what you're getting.

Jealousy, which acts as a clot in a Player Hater's heart, is a key explanation for their cattiness. Though it's never certain, usually bikini contests turn out some good-looking women. Even if they have "but-tafaces," which is when everything looks good "but her face," most of these women have toned bodies. If they didn't, they wouldn't compete. Every now and again, a contest will have a severely out-of-shape contestant, but in general, and definitely in high-caliber contests, the women are above average compared to the general population. And don't hate, because it's the truth!

Since these women look the way they do, they're used to everyone around them blowing smoke up their asses. They're used to being the prettiest around, and perhaps they are. That's until another gal walks up with a better boob job and longer extensions. If a gal's stomach is tighter, teeth are whiter, or ass is harder, then the green-eyed monster comes flying out of the cave! The fact that they are competing only throws more wood onto the fire. Should one jealous person not win, then the winner becomes the recipient of *a lot* of negative energy. Negative energy travels from one eye to another, so many contestants are subjected to the evil eye, whether they be giving or receiving it.

There's yet another log: Many times at local or collegiate contests, there is alcohol involved. I've seen bitches completely ripped onstage—one girl damn near broke her ankle in her stripper shoes! Imagine how heated things can get when girls are slurring their words and slamming down shots of cheap vodka.

The reason for fierce competition often stems from jealousy. Other contestants, however, have their own agendas. While some girls get trashed and rip their clothes off, some treat it like a business. They go in, they demolish, and they get the hell out. By the next day, they've packed up, paid the hotel bill, and traveled to the next city that's hosting a contest. They go in, collect the money, go for a run, and get a good night's rest. I have done it a few times, just jamming from city to city to earn a respective spot in the international competitions and, of course, to seriously rectify my cash flow problem. Geez, just talking about it makes me wanna enter one! My experiences could take forever to tell, and though they are quite entertaining when broken down to the core, we simply don't have enough trees on planet Earth to transcribe them all.

Bitch story: When I was a young little calf just starting my modeling career, I had to jump from city to city not only to win weekly competitions but also to beat out all the weekly winners combined if I wanted to take part in an international competition. I wasn't even sure what exactly the process entailed, but when I qualified for more than one final, I was pleased that I had scored a few chances to win a final and ultimately represent one of the venues.

I remember that I had smaller boobies back then, cupcakes, if you will. In one of my first contests, I didn't win first place. Even though I had a better body than the winner in that particular contest, it was obvious that her hooters outweighed mine by a long shot. I was irritated and acted quickly. I marched into my surgeon's office and had my boobies inflated to a healthy D. I resurfaced three weeks later and won the final! So, in essence, my boobs were free. The previous winner immediately noticed, and when I took off my robe, she quipped, "They're bigger than mine." They sure were!

Beauty pageants and bikini contests are breeding grounds for hate! I have witnessed this in the past, but as I've grown older, I see it in what I dare say as a comical perspective. As of this writing, the most recent contest I participated in was a real one to write home about! What a plethora of different personalities, morals, and goal setters! I have to set some ground rules about Bikini Bitches and their pageantry.

Foremost, like a good versus bad clothing store, at a contest, I can size up who's a threat and who's not. First: the face and hair. Some girls don't have pretty faces but can do their makeup well, complete with false lashes. Some girls also have bigger hair, which helps, but the most important thing is the length.

Second: Bathing suit. Does the color pop? I know blondes can be hard to beat if they're wearing pink, and brunettes if wearing red. I also look at the cut. If I think someone's a threat to me and she has a triangle bikini top on and a tiny tie-side bottom, I immediately look next to her body. Finally, the beauty of the face is considered. Because it's rare that judges will get an up-close appraisal, I don't weigh the face as heavily as I would in a beauty pageant.

I think there is a delicate balance with Bikini Bitches when it comes to being judged. You absolutely have to win the male vote, but what about the female vote? Female judges are bitches because they can be monkey wrenches in your program, the weakest link, if you will. This type of bitch is a Player Hater in a judge's body. In bikini contests, it's easier for a jealous judge to bar you from winning. She intervenes and grin at your loss; meanwhile, your electricity gets shut off. There have been instances when I felt I didn't win a bikini contest because of a female judge gone bitch, including times when another girl won because her girlfriend was on the panel. Sometimes judges act as Scrappy-Doos to certain contestants, scoring them very high and scoring you very low.

It's hard for club managers to control the rigging sometimes because some judges tell their friends to enter on the down low. Plus, they want chicks to enter because it brings business. Is it worth the gamble? It can be. I have taken the gamble and won; I have taken it and lost. Nevertheless, the show must go on.

Pageant

I've been in pageants all my life, and they're one of my areas of expertise. Being that I was a tender two-year-old when I won my first pageant, I didn't know diddly-squat about bitches. However, I started noticing after a while, I would say around four years old, something was going on. In other words, these packs of little ones and I weren't just modeling, smiling, and speaking into a microphone (yes, when I was that young!) for no reason. We were in a competition where bicycles, trophies, shiny sashes, and crowns were given as prizes. What a dream for a little girl … to be queen! I wanted these prizes and realized I had to compete to obtain them. Well, guess what. So did every other little girl on the stage. And even then, at that young age, we had an understanding that one of us was gonna win that Strawberry Shortcake bicycle. This was just the beginning.

At the time, I think the pageant moms were the bitchiest people in the auditorium. They would glare, stare, and get pissed when their daughters didn't win. They would harass judges afterwards, demanding to see scores (and in some instances, recount the scores!), all in the name of a crown, a bicycle, and to have their daughters in the newspaper. Talk about a catfight!

But as I grew older and developed more as a model and a contestant, I came into a new breed of contestants. We're talking some hard-core cutthroat Pageant Bitches. It takes years to develop a pageant skill unless you have a great coach that can mold you quickly, but these girls were like me—veterans—so to go head-to-head in a state or national competition was a tough call. What's more, the higher in the ranks one becomes in pageantry, the more you see the same faces. The circle becomes smaller, and you get used to competing against one another. Because I was climbing the ranks and learning the ropes of this new, more experienced group, I wasn't seen as a threat—yet. Moreover, I did notice a lot of iciness between some contestants. I also was snubbed by some because I wasn't quite yet a veteran. However, I learned over a good five-year span (and my goodness, I can't be sure how many competitions—probably sixty or so) that just because you were a veteran didn't mean you were going to be friends. You simply earned respect, and that was that.

It's a marvel, these pageants, because you always hear about "making friends and making memories."

Well, let me tell you, *very*, *very* rarely do you actually make friends with the others. Fake friends are what you make, and the memories of them can be nightmares. Cordial? Absolutely. You can't be standing there in rehearsal and be like, "You gross bitch, get away from me!"

You know what I find to be so true and intriguing? That 90 percent of those voted Miss Congeniality are the bitchiest ones and the ones you should look out for. They're either brand-new, absolutely clueless contestants or they're snakes in the grass—snakes I often wanted to strike with my high heel.

And having to associate at lunch was a horror because most of the time you're fed pizza and salty foods from the chow wagon (which is a no-no for donning a swimsuit). So you're there picking at your lettuce and throwing bread crumbs at yourself to pass the time before you burst and start hurling bread rolls at the Pageant Bitches. Lunchtime is the perfect time for us to "get to know each other and to bond," which really means question each other on what color our gowns are, what we are doing for talent, as well as swimsuit color—all that razzle-dazzle.

It's uncomfortable because a cardinal rule is never to reveal what you're wearing or what you're doing for talent. After a preliminary competition, I've seen girls freak out and change gowns based on another contestant's wardrobe. I've also seen others wear "pretend" gowns, and then come finals night, they change to their "real" gowns. And we're supposed to be friends. Right.

May I have a bread roll right now so I can gag on it? Thanks!

Even if all seems fine and friendly, there are a significant amount of jabs and passive-aggressive behaviors going on. And a lot of sabotage—like going to the dressing room and finding your gown ripped or the zipper glued. Or makeup or hairspray missing—things of that nature. Broken heels or jewelry is common. In most state pageants, you have to leave your items backstage, so often the chaperones are in the rehearsals as well, and if a contestant really wants to, she can excuse herself to the bathroom and do what she's gotta do. Terrible, isn't it? These bitches.

As far as passive-aggressive behavior, one tactic that I witnessed a lot was contestants telling other contestants that they "looked nervous" ... right before going into the interview room. That's why a lot of contestants wear headphones while waiting for interview—to block out the cattiness. I used to envision purple and white light around me and even project purple on the girls I thought wished me harm.

One of the worst contestants I ever dealt with was so nice when I was a newbie. And I actually liked her because at the time I was naive enough to believe she was a good person. But since I wasn't a threat to her, it was okay for her to be friendly. However, as time went on and I became strong, she shape-shifted into a complete Jack-in-the-Box Bitch. What popped out of her box was a monster. And it seethed, foamed out of the mouth, and spewed venom at me. Kind of like in *The Exorcist*, when she spews green shit at everyone. It wasn't puke this Pageant Bitch was spewing, okay? She was throwing out some crazy green shit.

Going head-to-head in quite a few pageants, I usually beat her, except for once. So naturally, when we competed again, there was a putrid toxicity in the air. Now, I'm a curvaceous type and buxom, whereas this bitch had a body like an ironing board. Nothing there—just what my mom described as mosquito bites for tits and an ironing board for an ass (she said it! I didn't!). My mom also told me, "You can dress a monkey in the finest silk suit, but the bottom line is it's still a monkey." As the old adage goes, "Mama knows best."

So here we were again at state, and I was in the public bathroom with my roommate behind the stage, getting ready for the swimsuit lineup (my roommate was a diamond—she was truly sweet). And in waltzed the bitch and went into the stall. My roommate was gluing my bathing suit down so my derriere would be kept under wraps, and she commented, "Girl, you got a booty on you." I really didn't mean for it to come out the way it did, but I said, "Yes, I'm glad it's not flat."

Oops! Next thing we knew, the stall door came flying open. It was the monster. But this time, she had grown wings, was breathing fire, and smoke was coming out of her ears and nose. The green shit was about to be expelled when she seethed, "I like my flat ass! At least it's not fake, like some people." To this day, I believe that she didn't spew too much because number one, she had nothing left to spew; and number two, she knew that what I was saying was innocent. But that will remain forever a mystery, a mystery hidden in her cave, where she spends all day doing God knows what. Just as a guide, the keys to handling Pageant Bitches are as follows:

- Remain cordial at all times
- Don't let them make you feel insecure with comments about your hair, clothing, body—or anything, for that matter
- Take insults as a form of flattery and fear on their part
- Keep your distance

Competing —much less winning— in a pageant is no easy feat. It's a competition—just like any other sport, right? Not really. Beauty queens are lovely because they articulate when speaking, engage in public relations, and serve as ambassadors of goodwill. They must be talented, educated, have great penmanship, and "save the world" in some way. Basically, you have to be Wonder Woman. The problem is that Wonder Women isn't a bitch. Strong in mind, body, and soul, but she's no bitch. And she isn't anyone's bitch either. In a sense, every day is like a pageant. So keep your head held high and defuse those bitches. If you do, you will be a winner *every day*, I promise.

Queen bitch story: I recall this particular pageant where I was aiming for the Grand Overall. What that meant was that out of fifteen separate competitions (such as swimsuit, sportswear, talent, evening wear, interview, and so forth), whichever contestant's score tallied up to the highest won the grand prize. You had to have the absolute highest score out of every baby, child, adolescent, teen, or miss contestant competing.

I had every area covered. I kicked ass and knew it. But there was this particular category that threw me for a loop: Best Costume. I had a great costume. I was a butterfly with enormous lavender wings. My wings had sparkly pastel shapes inside them, and I had a gorgeous purple head wrap and glittery stockings. My mom and I had spent days sewing, gluing, cutting, stitching, and stapling. We made a harness of wood so that the heavy wings would stay on securely. I tried it on a thousand times, and I'm surprised I never took flight!

When I stepped onstage for the Best Costume competition, I took one look at the panel and thought, *Oh, shit.* Even though I was just a fledgling, I knew a Player Hater when I saw one. My eyes studied the rest of the panel, and there they were: a group consisting of normal people who were in total admiration over me, the butterfly princess. I knew my costume was the best. My mother and I had crafted a gorgeous larger-than-life costume. It had sparkle, shine, and razzle-dazzle. It was spectacular! Our work was in vain, however. From the moment I locked eyes with the female judge, I knew I was in deep shit. This judge bitch seemed to be about my age. There she was, pen in hand, and as I slowly worked the runway, I had enough time to compute that she was a Hater.

If I had only been the second best costume, not the first, then she would have had mercy. *However*, because I was the best, she knew a second-place finish could have cheated me out of the overall crown. As I suspected, the bitch flexed her muscles. I remember coming offstage, and my mom was so proud.

"Honey, you were the best!"

I replied, "Thanks, Mom, but there was a jealous bitch on the panel!"

My mom's smile turned upside down, only to become a frown. I expressed my concerns to her about the Player Hater judge. After a few hours of pondering, an alarm sounded in my head. Like a dance of light, it hit me, and I knew I'd been correct to suspect a Player Hater. *It* was a memory, a true occurrence that did nothing but validate what my Inner Bitch had proposed all along. This bitch judge was a Player Hater indeed! I mentally investigated further, put two and two together, and remembered that I had competed with this judge in the past. She placed far behind me on the occasion, so of course she was as bitter as a winter wind chill.

I'm not going to go as far as saying she discriminated against me because I placed higher than she did in a past pageant. But one thing is for certain: she *did* see me that day, saw that I was the best, and reveled in her position of power. There she sat, carefully scanning each contestant, only to make a few notes with her mighty blue Bic pen, compliments of the Sheraton. The minute she discerned me, she made the conscious decision to score me very low.

I knew she would. I told my mom the same thing right before I stepped down the last step. I could've doubted my instincts. I could've doubted my costume. But I knew damn well that the costume was just too much for anything but first place. There was too much fabric; too much glitter; too many sequins, stitches, and hardware involved. Nevertheless, when it came to the day of crowning, I was flabbergasted that I didn't even make runner-up in costume! It ended up being the one competition in which I did not place. It was so overtly foul, and the fact that I placed in

Talent only verified my suspicions. I am very honest, and I promise you this: If I took home Talent, you bet your britches I should've walked away with Best Costume. This bitch, whom I can't name thanks to slander, played a factor in the whole shebang!

Luckily, they dropped the lowest score, so despite this canker sore, I still won the overall. It was such a large pageant that one category was just a dent in the overall tally, but I'm certain it was close. I walked away with a cash prize, a three-foot crown, and a trophy so big it consumed our entire Jeep!

Bar

Let's get two things straight before we learn how to identify this bitch: First, let it be said that there are all different types of bars: college bars, hotel bars, tiki bars, nightclub bars, and restaurant bars (even mainstream places such as Outback Steakhouse and Applebee's). The second thing? Not one of these places is immune to the bitches that exist in this world. The interesting thing about the bar environment is that you will have a regular person (who may have a bitch characteristic or two compounded, also known as a Binary Bitch) who, when exposed to said environment, has her bitch qualities come out.

Bar bitches are an interesting lot because their bitch traits only come out in a bar environment. Whether it's ordering a drink in a fast-paced environment such as a hot spot nightclub, a bluesy-woozy jazz club, a Las Vegas casino, or the tiki bar at Hooters, beware! You're going to run into a Bar Bitch. There are three types of Bar Bitches:

1) The ones sitting or standing at the bar
2) The ones behind the bar
3) The ones that are dancing *on* the bar

In a crowded nightclub, it can be difficult to wedge your way between two or three bitches standing at a bar in an effort to place an order, and the level of bitchiness can easily escalate depending on how much (and of what) the bitches at the bar have consumed. Make the wrong eye contact, accidentally bump arms, hips, or booty, and you can easily have an altercation, especially if the bitch has a sidekick wing bitch, otherwise known as a "Scrappy-Doo."

What's more, if a guy is eyeing you or men in general are wanting to put you on a plate and devour you like a Rooty Tooty Fresh N' Fruity (with hot chocolate on the side), it's very easy for the Bar Bitches to become engorged with jealousy and hate, which often leads to problems. Remember, bitch attitudes are almost always derived from hate. You best put some sage where the sun don't shine (as in your bra, panties, or the zip pocket of your purse) because Bar Bitches, despite the similarity of their strength in regard to the other bitches in their tier of the hierarchy, are a real pain in the booty.

The reason they're a pain in the booty is because they want to control the bar space, as this is where they obtain the most attention. Control. Attention.

Ego. There's a pattern when it comes to bitches, and the Bar Bitch is no exception. These bitches fall in the Hierarchy of Bitches where they all look the same—like clones but in different situations. This makes them even more baffling as far as bitch characteristics are concerned. Here are some key traits:

- The hogging of space at the bar. Arms on the bar, a straddle of the legs, or purses on the bar or slung over their shoulders to take up as much space as possible.
- Ass out. This is a subliminal message to back off. If the booty is perched outward to where it's a distraction, then this bird is ready for a fight for bar space.
- Snake eyes. A stare down is an animal instinct.

Bar Bitches are thirsty animals. For attention, they order drinks with olives on a stick. Maybe even those juicy white miniature onions on plastics swords. How to handle? If it's a crowded bar, the first thing to do is try to find an opening next to a man (preferably two) and ask politely if you can squeeze in. They will probably oblige. If there isn't a whole lot of room but a bundle of chaos, you'll have to put on your night vision and find the quickest route to the bar whilst avoiding the Bar Bitches. Remember, they want the same thing you do—to order—and in addition, they want the attention.

So avoid physical contact at all times with the Bar Bitch. Rubbing elbows with men? Fine. Bar bitches? No.

If a collision seems imminent with a Bar Bitch, compliment her. Excuse yourself and compliment her somehow. Say you like her necklace, shirt, whatever. Pick something and tell her so. If it's a desolate bar, you can always strike up a conversation if you're getting snake eyes. And then buy her a drink or a shot (works like a charm!). The other type of Bar Bitch is a bitch bartender. If the bartender sizes you up and feels you are competition physically (for instance, your hair is longer or you have bigger boobs), the person may ignore you repeatedly just to make you wait … even if you were there before other people. I'll be honest: that type of crap works my nerves. I know what they're doing, and they know it too. And it's a control issue—one of the cardinal traits of any bitch. You're at their mercy for a drink, a bowl of nuts, or three olives on a stick. And the abuse of power is sickening.

As for the Behind-the-Bar Bitch, tipping well is a surefire way to cease the bitch attitude and get immediate assistance, especially in a busy atmosphere. And that makes perfect sense. Depending on the regulations of the establishment, you can even offer to buy a shot for the bartender. Some will sneak one in, and some places allow it to a minimum if it builds rapport with a patron.

I find that buying a shot for a Bar Bitch subdues him or her, as counterproductive as this may seem. If a person is at a bar, then he or she is there to drink, so why would the person turn down free alcohol? It gives a sense of camaraderie—and before you know it, you'll become each other's wing bitches. I've witnessed this phenomenon on numerous occasions, and that's the only reason I advise it.

You'll know Bar Bitches when you see them because they have this energy field around them—bitch barriers, if you will. But they can be easily transcended and defused, and you never know: you may end up with a new friend. It just depends on the circumstances, plain and simple. You're entitled to have fun while you're out, and if you find yourself in a pickle, take a shot and buy the other person a shot. If not, steer clear and "squeeze in." Cheers!

Gym

One would think that going to the gym would help blow off steam. Not necessarily true. Yes, going to the gym is important, and yes, many people exercise there. Some women are built like a brick house and are in super good shape. A gym has many of those women. A gym has many of those women, a gym has many of those women, except they're built like a "bitch house." In addition, the gym environment is a big brick bitch house because within the environment are different types of sub-bitches. Here they are, listed in all their glory:

- Show-off Bitches
- Do-Nothing Bitches
- Stinky and Sweaty Bitches
- Don't-Take-My-Floor-Space Bitches

Okay, let's start with the Show-Off Bitches since they're so showy and have to be number one and all that jazz. These bitches have great bodies and show them off—and how. I think there's a disturbingly huge amount of "Look at me, look at me. *I said look at me, dammit!*" type of mentality going on. I think it's important to be kept together and look tidy at the gym, wearing regular nice gym clothes because you're forced to face yourself in a lot of mirrors, but these bitches are extreme. They wear shorts so short that you may as well not even call them shorts. Sports bras are the only acceptable boob coverage (hey, tank tops are for losers y'all—get with the program!). All of this wrapped up in one fabulous spray tan package with a dab of hot pink lip gloss and the girl is on *fire*! Mission accomplished. Yes, we are looking at you. We are also looking at how you turn your nose up as you literally suck the life out of your Evian bottle. I don't think these bitches even look at themselves. They just want you to look at them showing off. How to handle? Just look at them, for goodness' sake, and give them what they want, because you won't be able to not look since they are so overt … but just for a few seconds. And keep on working out! Next!

Okay, these next types of bitches make me laugh and cringe at the same time. They take all this time to get dressed, get in the car, waste gas, sign into the gym, and then they do "abs"-so-"glute"-ley *nada*! They are totally nomadic herders. They wander around, pondering which machine to use, move like turtles, grab some water, peer into the aerobics room—anything and everything to avoid doing *something*. What makes them bitches is because they are so stupid. I don't cover stupid bitches in this book, but if I did, this would be a prime example. It's like, okay, *what* may I ask are you doing? Nothing.

Seeing them squeeze out a few crunches or two minutes on the StairMaster is like watching a rare lunar eclipse. Before you know it, they've left the gym, and what's scary is that they probably think they've actually done something! How to handle? Well, you certainly could ask them if they're lost or need assistance (you never know, clueless birds that they are) or you can always discreetly point them out to a trainer and have him or her approach the bitches. The reason these types are bitches is because they waste space and energy by even observing them. Give the person a helping hand and point him or her in the right direction. And make the bitch drop and give you twenty!

Of all the nastiness in this world of bitches, the Sweaty and Stinky Bitch is one is the greasiest. Granted, the gym bitch types are all by-products of the mother ship, but even so, this one is the literally the greasiest physically.

It is absolutely revolting when you are waiting for a machine and when you finally get your chance, there's an icky slathering of sweat on it. O-M-G. Gross! Some higher-end gyms have towel service, which I think all gyms should be required to have, from a sterile perspective. However, other gyms (such as some apartment complexes and other ones that I can't name) leave it up to the patron to bring their own towels.

Now let's talk about towels. One great way to handle these revolting entities is to bring two towels, one for you and one for the greasy, *plus* a disinfectant spray or mist of some sort.

Simply mist down the bench or machine after the person is done, and if need be, wipe it down. This isn't to suggest that you need a hard-core aerosol spray that comes out like you're using a fire extinguisher. Just a simple disinfectant will do. Try a clean laundry scent—nothing too heavy to upset the, ahem, cleaner patrons.

I've worked as a personal trainer in the past, in Florida as well as New York, and we were taught as part of our certification to be aware of patrons who are careless with their sweating and cleaning up after themselves. It sounds like a no-brainer, but these careless, greasy bitches exist.

And they *are* bitchy because they have no respect for anyone else, much less the gym and the equipment. A gym towel is a towel, not a sweaty shirt or a tissue.

Aside from protecting yourself with your clean linen spray and a backup towel, remember that you shouldn't have to clean up after someone else. So if you're the ballsy type, say to this person as soon as he or she gets off the machine, "Excuse me, I need to use that machine, but I can't with the way you just left it. Do you have a towel?" The person will say no. To which you reply, "Well, please do something about it because I need to get my workout on and I can't use this machine until you fix this situation."

What is the person going to say? The bitch has to! You may even offer a suggestion: "They sell towels at the front desk. Will you buy one and start using it today?" If they do in fact sell them. If they don't sell them, simply whip out your own and say, "Well, here's an extra one with a little disinfectant. Will you please clean it?"

And the bitch *should*. If he or she is being rude (or on steroid rage), don't hesitate to get management involved. No excuses! If you go to the gym and realize that you don't have a towel, modify your workout or go to a class. Just don't be a stink bomb and let others suffer the aftermath. Truly, because I can't deal today with that nonsense.

Don't-Take-My-Floor-Space Bitches are extremely territorial. The gym can be a jungle indeed. I guess that's why when we were growing up, they called those metal and wooden playground things "jungle gyms." Ever go to a gym class and you find a bunch of bitches right in the front of the door, pacing around like lions in a cage? When the door opens, they charge forth while you scramble, only to realize they have secured the mirror with the best view, the best weights, and the best weighted body bars. Why do you think that is? Well, often it's because they demand it with their presence. They are on task, on time (if not early), and know what type of weight they literally need to pull. Well, it can be quite annoying when you need a certain weight and you end up having to either compromise your weight *or* stand way in the back where you can't even see yourself. Or worse yet, secure a weird spot where you may end up donkey kicking someone (or getting donkey kicked) during cardio.

Same with the yoga enthusiasts, who are deemed the most peaceful of all gym patrons, as if they were the Dalai Lama; they get *so* pissed when you take their favorite spots. So much that they want to roll up their yoga mats and smack you in the face with them. When they meditate and sit Indian-style with their eyes closed, if you come in late, they open one eye widely and *hate* you for destroying their moment of tranquility. Well, at least they have good floor space, right? Twist yourself into a pretzel, bitch, and get over it already!

The only true way to handle such a bitch is to let your Inner Bitch be known. Figure out what weight you need to pull in advance, what height of step you need in advance, and what weight body bar you need in advance. And decide where you would like to stand on the floor. I had an instance once at a very popular sports club, where I knew what I needed to obtain my perfect pump. I also knew what position in the room I desired. This Gym Bitch (who as a regular, I could see was somewhat of a bully) got in my face because I had the position she wanted—but I had beaten her to the punch (no pun intended).

She threw a mini-tantrum. Do you want to know how I defused her? Looking her squarely in the eye, I forcefully released my twelve-pound weights out of my palms without flinching, cocked my right brow, and put my hands on my hips. My body language told her to *back off, bitch*. And she did. And she had to spend the rest of the class looking at my ass do the around the world on the step. So, please!

You don't need to deal with anyone that tries to control you; we know that by now. But as I said, bitches are *e-vuh-ree-where*. So keep healthy and fit but let your Inner Bitch throw on those boxing gloves when you face a challenge!

Authority Bitches

Ahhhh, wouldn't it be nice even for just one day to not feel controlled, be controlled, or have someone trying to control you? What a sweet day that would be. Unfortunately, "control" scenarios happen so much in our daily lives that they're hard to avoid. What's more, sometimes we don't even realize they're happening. Worst-case scenario? We feel we can't regain control.

With Authority Bitches, "control" is the name of the game, and because we are forced to deal with them often (sometimes more than once on any given day), they can, well, control how your days go. Some even have so much power that if you rub them the wrong way, they can set you up on a butterfly effect that can take some time to cease. These bitches are tricky types because on the surface it looks as if you have to kiss their asses just to get by. These bitches show up in the form of abusive bankers, hotel staff, supervisors of any kind, and security like those you find in airports.

They're difficult because of their amazingly overinflated egos combined with the high that they get from their obnoxious abuse of power. What troubles me most about these bitches is that they can be authorities in manipulative mental behavior. I can crack a whip as my Inner Bitch sees fit, but this one requires a crystal whip and a leash. And horse blinders. But with the right words and the right way to plead a case, these bitches can be turned around. Here is how to identify Authority Bitches: They have the power to deny you something that you need or desire. They usually say no at first when you present them with a request. They tend to speak in terms of policies, rules, and regulations. They show a strong lack of sympathy, empathy, or any type of emotion, for that matter. If they feel threatened, they can—and usually do—make the request even tougher to achieve.

For instance, I was once coaching at a beauty pageant and was asked on a date that same night. It was a Saturday, and I couldn't get to the bank on time, so I asked my mom to please do me a favor and make the deposit I needed to get my hair done. If you knew how frazzled I get coaching, you would see how imperative it was. Otherwise, the date would have taken me for the Bride of Frankenstein and not a potential bride-to-be.

Because I was actually at the pageant, I had my debit card, but no checkbook. So I called up the bank to see if my mom could simply deposit the cash and voila! The bitch on the phone sneered, "No. We can only accept deposits with your full account number." Gag! I explained to her the situation, and she again sneered, saying no. Ugh! I knew in my heart of hearts that there was a way. With the image of the Bride of Frankenstein running through my head, I asked, "Well then, how do I obtain the account number in this situation?" She replied that I needed Internet access. Being one step ahead, I told her I had already looked up my account on my iPad. She instructed me to log back on and look in a certain area and it would be there.

I made her promise that was true, as I had to get back to the auditorium, and I did as told when back in the audience. When I saw a set of numbers on the account site, I thought, *Aha!* Because I was in the audience, I didn't want to be a rude bitch, so I quickly jotted down the numbers and texted my mom those numbers.

After the pageant, my phone rang, and my mom was on the line. The Authority Bitch on the phone hadn't known what she was talking about. Those numbers I wrote down were my debit card numbers, *not* my bank account. Sigh. I hate wasting time, and that bitch wasted mine! So long story short, my mom politely explained the situation to the branch manager, and they allowed her to make the cash deposit;

to me, not being able to without an account number is stupid. I definitely can see withdrawals and other at-risk transactions, but cash money? Please! As if someone is just going to go in a bank and drop money in my account for his or her health.

The moral of the story is that by being polite and essentially kissing ass, we accomplished what we needed to. They didn't have to allow it, but both the phone operator and the branch were in an authoritative position. Ugh. In case you're wondering, the date went well, but he wasn't my type. But I definitely didn't look like the Bride of Frankenstein. Oh, the horror!

Another story about an Authority Bitch happened to a boyfriend of mine. This one is a classic. He was visiting Florida, where his mother lives, and while he was there, he had an emergency and had to call for an ambulance. When he went back to California, his mom later informed him that the bill had arrived at her house, meaning he would have to call his insurance company to report it.

When he did call, he gave the agent his insurance number on the card, explained what had happened with the address misunderstanding, and gave his address in California. The agent then asked him what his mother's address was, which he told her. However, she also wanted the zip code, which he didn't have on hand because he was on his way to work (using a Bluetooth, of course). He was trying to recall but was a number off, so the agent told him she could not complete his request. He asked her, "Not even with my insurance card number?"

"No!" she snapped.

He replied, "Listen, lady, do you want to get paid or not?"

"Well, we can't process it without proper identity with the zip code," she quipped.

He was beside himself. "Do you honestly think someone else is going to pay *my* insurance? Like someone is just going to call up and pretend to be me and pay it, right? And that person has everything but a zip code, right?"

After some bantering back and forth, she finally let go of her control and used her authority in a positive way by letting the transaction go through. There are three keys to defusing an Authority Bitch:

1) Patience
2) Reasoning
3) Resilience

Let's first discuss the virtue of patience. Patience with these bitches is important because often they keep you waiting in line (and they're often long lines) … at the bank, the post office, the airport, and such. If it's not a long line, they simply keep you waiting—much like waiting to speak to your boss, waiting for a job interview, or finding out if you've been approved for a car loan. Also, telephone calls to credit card companies and the like seem to take a very long time due to automated service and hold times.

Granted, the length of wait is partially determined by the number of people also waiting, but also how quickly the potential bitches assist in moving things along. I have found that if the potential bitches are as slow as molasses (and therefore don't move their asses), the more likely they will be moody and not have a care in the world about their attitudes.

You may grow impatient waiting for people you need to handle business with, but please don't. The reason is that if they're going to be bitches because they don't care, fuming will do you no good because they simply don't care. If, on the other hand, they're in a positive mood and you wait and wait and complain when you finally get to speak to them, you're going to turn their smile upside down and they won't be as keen to help you. In fact, if they take offense to you, they may not help you at all and you're back to square one. If you a pitch a fit after that and managers get involved, the whole situation can go bitch and you may be denied service completely. Then you're *really* back to square one. So always remember to have patience!

Next, you must know how to reason with the person who has the authority. For instance, let's say you want to extend your stay for a few hours at a hotel and they say you must check out by noon, per their policy. You could say something like, "I'm aware of your policy and thank you for your hospitality, but my flight has been delayed several hours and it would be gracious of you to allow me the room for a little longer." Never demand it, never say until such and such o'clock; simply give the reason. They may ask you how long, but simply ask what the absolute latest is. Reason with them. Perhaps you ate something in their dining room that was spoiled and you've been vomiting all morning. Something like 99 percent of the time, they will say yes because hotels do not want sick guests—and certainly not ones who are sick from eating in their dining room. I'm not necessarily saying to say these things, but the point is, you have reasoned with them. They have the control, remember, so always be gracious and reason.

The same goes for credit card companies, with which reasoning can resemble negotiation. Reason that you've been a customer for years, you've told others to sign up, that you need this favor or this action taken because of the circumstances. Remember too that often people with control and what seems like "power" can be reasoned with because they get off on being able to make the decision to help you out or not. And usually they will, if you're polite. You'll be on the phone about to smash a Budweiser can on your forehead and crush it because you feel like you're kissing major ass, but let me ask you a question: are you getting what you want or not? The situation will get resolved eventually (usually sooner if you don't crush the can), and then you can go about your day with the feeling that you obtained your goal.

Finally, we have the element of resilience. With resilience comes the Inner Bitch. If you're not getting what you want, speak up! Don't complain but speak up. If you've been patient, reasoned with the bitch, and have been gracious, all to no avail, simply move on. Go to a different bank branch or thank the bitch on the line and hang up. Then call back and try again with someone else. If you feel that you're being treated wrong by a bitch, then don't ask the bitch for the manager. Go to another associate and politely ask for the manager. In fact, often managers are happy to help.

But beware! They too are definitely Authority Bitches, so you don't go up to them red-faced and arms waving and bitching yourself. Use tact, poise, and graciousness, explain your problem, listen to what they have to say, and go from there. If they help you on the spot, great! Take it and cease. *But* depending on how offensive the original bitch was, you might want to get the manager's business card and send a thank-you e-mail (or get the business e-mail if the bitch episode occurred over the phone) and then point out in the letter that the Authority Bitch wasn't very helpful and that the customer service wasn't up to par. You were so disappointed and the experience wasted your time, the bitch's time, and the manager's time. You can play with the theatrics and make the letter nice and vivid but always remember what Mama Erika Valdez has taught you: patience, reasoning, and resilience.

Binary and Super

A Binary Bitch is a two-part combination, such as a Jack-in-the-Box Player Hater, Boob-Envying On-the-Job, or Swag-Wag Male Bitches, and so forth. If you're having difficulty discerning what type of bitch someone is being, it's quite possible that that person is a Binary Bitch. Much like a binary star, these bitches' qualities orbit around a common center (themselves, or as in astronomy, the *barycenter*.) If you can identify at least one of the bitch traits, then work it from that angle first. Hopefully you'll be able to see a common thread and then out will pop the other one still in orbit.

At the very worst, someone can actually be three bitches in one, such as a Jack-in-the-Box On-the-Job Player Hater. Ouch! Bitch combos—these are super-sized! These triple bitches are no fun and are over-whelming to tackle. It can be done, but depending on their threefold combination, you should question whether to keep the connection, especially when one of the traits is a Player Hater. However, if you have, for instance, a Jack-in-the-Box Meet-You-Halfway Bailout Bitch, then there's hope for the relationship.

Identifying Binary and Super Bitches can be difficult because they throw so many characteristics around. What's more, one trait may stronger than the other (or others), which makes the bitches appear as if they're only one type. Then—*drumroll, please*—other bitch characteristics start to emerge, thus making them even more difficult to defuse. There's always hope, but sometimes the negative outweighs the positive. This is something you must contemplate and give good thought to: how heavy is their bitch negativity?

If you suspect someone could be more than one type of bitch, ask yourself what was the worst behavior you have ever seen that person display. Write it down. Write down the next worst behavior until you lead up to the best behavior you have seen him or her display. This will help you see the severity of the bitchiness and help you to decide whether the person is truly a Binary or Super Bitch or simply had an episode or two of bitchy behavior. Once thoughts are on paper, you'll be able to see the bitch price tag more clearly.

If the price is overbearing and more than you think you can spiritually afford, pass on the person and redirect yourself somewhere else. There are too many bitches in the galaxy for you to be consumed by one Binary or Super Bitch. A Binary Bitch here and there, okay, but be aware of who is sucking your energy and remember to protect yourself. If you can defuse bitches rapidly one by one, the easier life will become for us all.

Li'l Bitches

Selfie

Dumb

Cosmetic Counter

Dump Their Shit on You

Scopers

Pushy

She Has the Man I Want

Selfie

Damn bitch gets on my nerves big time. Folks, we have learned by now that ego is almost always somehow involved with bitches. The more ego, the more bitch. And this one is probably one of the worst (and current) types of egotistical bitches I've seen. And guess what. You most likely have seen this type too. That's because they take ridiculous pictures of themselves all day and post them on social media: the Selfie Bitch.

If you speak German, great. "Was fur eine Schesse ist es, Joe?" If you don't know German, that means, "What the fuck is up, Joe? Come back from the bar!" I use that phrase as a reminder that people need to come back to reality. And if you notice, most women have these bitchy/smug/trying-to-be-sexy looks in their selfies, and it's all just so egotistical that it gives new meaning to the word ridiculous. And most women who take these selfies *are* bitches because they think the world revolves around them and they're so fabulous that everyone has to see them with a pile of makeup on in a sports bra in what probably is a Photoshopped-to-death photo anyway. Because aside from taking selfies constantly, they spend their time getting ready for them so they can Photoshop them.

If you're busy taking pictures of your ass or tits in hopes that you can gather a fan base, fine. That doesn't convince me much, however. If you have a business or something worthwhile to promote, you can become popular (I guess that's a choice word) with selfies. If you're doing it *all day*, *every night*, *all the time*, you need to kick back because you're missing out on life. Look, there is nothing wrong with taking pictures of your friends or family, or having someone take a picture of you after you win your Oscar for Best Actress. I get that. Special moments in life, cool.

But I'm keeping it real! If you're a professional model taking legitimate pictures, this is okay. But if you're just wasting time, you're being a self-absorbed bitch. Stop wasting your time and do something productive. Go get a college degree (or another one), take voice lessons, or go to the kitchen and make a sausage omelet. Go to the Grand Canyon. What's scary is that you will take selfies of yourself making the omelet at the Grand Canyon as you sing about your new college degree. So self- absorbed, by God! My reasoning is that eventually your ta-tas are going to be down at your knees or, for men, your balls will be. Where will your selfie fans be then? You will be thrown forever into obscurity in a selfie-absorbed world, and no one except you will remember that you ever posted a picture of yourself. Wait a tick … On that note, will you please send me those selfies when your ta-tas are on your knees so I can be amused? Then maybe you'll get a reprieve from me. I'll make a deal with you … I'll take one of me too, and you can have it bronzed for posterity. Deal? Yeah, right!

At that point, you will then look at how hot you once were (whether or not people ever thought that in the first place), and you will cry because the great, beautiful you will be absolutely forgotten (unless you become productive and love others besides yourself—then you will not be forgotten). And this all ties into if you're even remembered right now. There are so many dang selfies going around that I can't keep my head on straight, especially because most chicks look the same in them—and so do the guys—and if I see that stupid pouty lip expression with a look in your eyes as if you just had a salmon shoved up your ass *one more time* … Well, I just don't know what I'll do. I'll figure something out, anything but puke.

That's why it's important to look in the mirror—well, that's not actually good advice because many selfies are taken looking in a mirror except that you're standing backward with your phone (or something—I don't know). I took one once and couldn't see anything except my ass hanging out of my dress due to trying to get the right angle by leaning forward. I tried a couple of more times to do it like some of the selfie-obsessed do, but it wasn't working. Then I turned and looked in the mirror head-on and asked myself what the hell I was doing. I was wasting time. I'd rather take a power nap than take a selfie.

It's easy to have someone take a snapshot of you if that's what you really want. But what do you really see with the selfies? There's something different about having a photo of you taken by someone else while out and about, although I do think walking around asking people to take random photos of you for no good reason is strange. And that's why people take them themselves, so they can get up close and do the boobs pushed together, duck pout, and salmon-up-the-ass eyes look (or are in bathing suits and gym clothes). And I think if it were the other way, people would be kind of embarrassed because it's silly. I have big boobies too, but I'm actually giving you advice to not waste time photographing them and uploading them to a bunch of strangers. All day. All night. Every week. Every month. Because looks don't last forever.

So how do we handle this very annoying trend? Well, let me begin by saying that I feel this is an epidemic sweeping very young girls at an alarming rate—girls as young as twelve or as soon as they get their hands on a cell phone or tablet so they can access social media. Another facet to this complete monster is that it is being encouraged by women as a good thing, as if suggesting that being hot yet full of ego is a cool thing. In addition, celebrities are also pushing the problem on everyone. To make matters worse? Nine out of ten times, these selfies come across as sexually suggestive, with all the makeup, the facial expressions, and the showing of the body. And that's not just women! Men also are stripping down to their boxers and no shirts and … Good grief! Really? Really?!

So my first piece of advice if you see young people doing this is to explain that while it's great to take care of looks, education is extremely important and these selfies can damage their reputations—especially if posted on any social media such as Facebook, Instagram, Twitter, and whatever else could be out there. If they don't listen, take away all access to social media until you make sure they get the point. How people handle their children is their business, but this selfie shit is detrimental to reputation and learning. Period.

As for adults, if you see Selfie Bitches who have a problem with constantly taking photos of themselves, you should question what kind of people they are. I say that because obviously their egos are out of control. Either that or the bitches have no self-esteem, and both are sad traits. If you're convinced that it's an ego thing (which will be easy because they will highly likely possess other bitch qualities discussed in this book), you will have to ask yourself if these people are really worth your time. If you believe so, you'll have to talk to them about why they do it so much and plant the seed in their minds that time can be better spent in their lives.

You can point out how vain it is and use reverse psychology, saying, "Rather than constantly taking pictures of yourself, I'd like to spend more quality time with you." Or you can explain that you'd like to get to know them better inside instead of always seeing the outside. By all means, *do not* let them try to show you any of their selfies on social media or convince you to start taking them.

And celebrities? Puh-leeze. If you are looking at celebrity selfies—people you absolutely don't know—then you're wasting an incredible amount of time. And that would be everything that this bitch boils down to. A waste of time. Now, before I waste any more time talking about this selfie garbage, I'm moving on to our next bitch. Next!

Dumb

Have you ever been out on a date or in public with someone and that person starts acting a fool, appearing almost alien-like? Almost to the point where you want to deny you even know him or her? You're left shaking your head left to right in slow motion, thinking, *You dumb bitch*.

Let's get a few things straight regarding Dumb Bitches. Yes, they are dumb. Some people pretend to be dumb in order to actually gain control of a situation by drawing attention to themselves (twisted but true), and other people are just dumb. There really isn't a lot of substance or intellect behind Dumb Bitches, hence the name. In fact, they may think they're smart, but their level of idiocy is so high that they have intellectual delusions of grandeur.

They are also tacky. Boisterous and loud in public, they have zero tact when asking questions of others and are just sloppy in general. The Dumb Bitch really comes to life when drinking too much alcohol (outside of the home environment in particular). Granted, most people are also in danger of losing their marbles if they drink too much at home, but something about the outside world snatches the Dumb Bitches up, turns them inside out, and then launches them into a tree like toilet paper, as some immature fraternity boys do for fun. Not a good look.

What's terrible about them is that you normally don't find out that they're Dumb Bitches until you actually go out in public with them. At home? Perfectly normal. In the car? Just as so. A restaurant? Not so much. A bar? Fucking forget it! It is a wonder why (and how) someone could go from seemingly being cool as a cucumber to Dumb Bitch status depending on the environment. Folks, I gave this a lot of thought. I know when I'm dealing with a Dumb Bitch, but in the past, I pondered on the how and why. This is what I have come up with.

It seems the more people are around, the more likely the Dumb Bitch is going to show the need for attention. I have noticed these types are often alone (geez, I wonder why?), so when they *do* go out and garner some type—any type—of attention, their personalities become amplified in a negative way and the more thirsty they become for said attention. When it comes to attention, it really doesn't matter after a certain point if they are receiving it. If they are receiving it, they want more. If they aren't getting it, they want it even more. Twisted bitches they are indeed.

Concerning the Dumb Bitch, there is a section of the brain that actually controls a large part of the actions we take: the frontal lobe, which is one of the four major lobes. This particular lobe houses most of our dopamine-sensitive neurons that correspond with reward and attention (amongst other things). The Dumb Bitch is lacking in this section. That's not to suggest the person has brain damage, which is a serious and unfortunate condition, but something in this part of the brain is a bit "off." The frontal lobes involve the ability to recognize future consequences resulting from current actions, to choose between good and bad actions (or better and best), as well as override and suppress socially unacceptable responses. It's their behavior that makes them Dumb Bitches because, again, they require a certain amount of attention—even if they can't decide what kind, and I have found this manifests itself in an out-of-home environment. Typically it results in embarrassment for many people involved—with or without any alternate substance. The frontal lobe is also largely responsible for judgment, decision-making skills, attention span, and inhibition, making the Dumb Bitch a wild child as well!

I had a particular friend who was a little wild at home, but once we stepped out in public—usually at our favorite restaurants or whilst shopping—her personality changed. She was very loud, spoke in a high-pitched tone, and would even shriek from time to time. People would turn and look with expressions of, "What the heck is she all about?"

She was a friend, so I stuck around, but the dramatic way her personality would change from literally getting out the door to our destination was sometimes worrisome and baffling. I'm not her mother, but I would have to hush her at times or override her in a conversation just to make sure she didn't come across as ... well, honestly, like a Dumb Bitch.

There was that certain need for attention, and I noticed that by the way she would play with textures or tones in her voice as well as the way she told a story or simply discussed things. When she would slam on tables to make a point or laugh so loudly that the entire Los Angeles area could hear her, I wanted to crawl in my purse, hide behind my napkin, or simply go home. And I will not discuss going to a nightclub ... I hope you get the point.

So how do you handle such bitches? This is tough, but I suggest doing things one-on-one: going to the beach (when it's not crowded), going for a walk in a desolate park, renting a movie (not going to see one!), or making a meal at home.

If you do go out in public and the acting out starts, you must admit to the person that you are embarrassed and say that he or she needs to shush up and focus or you're cutting the cord on the day's events.

Explain that the bitch is acting like a fool and coming across stupid and immature. You're doing everyone a favor, trust me.

It can be hard to point these things out to people in a calm, nice way, but it can be done. You can also wait until you're alone with them but first tell them you care about them, yet what they did in public was humiliating to the way others perceived them as well as to you. And perhaps try to go out again, but … Nah, scratch that idea and keep it at home. Play chess, read to each other, learn something outside of the attention-seeking world the bitch longs for. If you give this person chance after chance and keep getting embarrassed in public, you might be a Dumb Bitch yourself. So crack the whip!

If it's only happened once, fine. Not everyone is a Dumb Bitch. But repeat offenders? No way, Jose. Now go to Toys "R" Us and get that chess game—just don't take the bitch with you!

Cosmetic Counter

The essence a department store delivers is one-stop shopping combined with ease and a hint of luxury. You can shop at your convenience without being hassled, try on the garments in convenient dressing rooms, and, when ready, make your purchase at the nearest register. With the illustrious lights, smells of fine fragrances in the air, and the cases of designer cosmetics, it can be a glamorous and exciting scene.

But consider the overwhelming, massive, mind-sweeping array of cosmetic counters occupying the floor space. If you're anything like I am, you like this fancy shit and belong to the designer cosmetic clientele. After all, the quality of the product is better and the packaging is more durable. What's more, you can play with or collect disposable samples before buying. Pull that stunt in most drugstores across America and you've just committed a crime, my friend. If you take your time at cosmetic counters and make smart choices, you're sure to stumble along items that you'll no doubt treasure for life.

With this beauty extravaganza comes a sense of responsibility as well as self-direction. I may be a beginner at some things, but I have a black belt when it comes to shopping. Even I, *Miss Fashionista*, have felt and lived through the overwhelming sense of anxiety that cosmetic counters can ignite. I'm at the point where I know what I need and from which brand, but I'll admit that even I put off going to the counters at times. I'll hold out for quite a while, but even when I am most prepared, I still never truly want to go there. Buying makeup is an odd transaction because you're required to come face-to-face with the most nostalgic piece of the department store phenomenon: the Cosmetic Counter Bitch.

It can be intimidating when you're in need of makeup magic and the magician behind the counter isn't as receptive as you'd hoped. Though sales associates can be helpful and kind, I have often found a measure of snottiness in the cosmetic department. Cosmetic Counter Bitches can't help but scope you out, and they do it in a couple of different ways. As you approach, they quickly summarize your entire financial history. What kind of clothes are you wearing? What about your shoes? Do you need to cut your hair? The answers to these questions project a magic number of how many dollars you can spend.

I remember that when I first became a client of Chanel, the saleswomen didn't see it coming. After all, I was only fourteen at the time, yet there was something very alluring about the Chanel counter. There I was—young, impressionable, and ready for makeup. They sold me all sorts of potions and creams, from foundation primers to lip liners (including one I'm still addicted to twenty years later: nude.) I guess they thought I was lots of fun too because I'd pay them a visit and let them paint and powder my face—and then buy it all! They didn't suspect, because of my age, that I was a live wire. Looks can be deceiving.

A Cosmetic Counter Bitch may also scope you out due to vanity. In order to work in such a department, one has to possess a certain measure of it. These people are constantly looking at themselves and paying attention to not only how they look but also how their *makeup* looks. They can't help but scope out you and your makeup and then compare it with themselves. It's probable that your makeup won't look as precise as theirs, so they're easily satisfied mentally and will proceed to help you. If your makeup is stellar, then for whatever reason, vanity strikes again and they'll take a liking to you. As odd as it may sound, beauty likes beauty. But whether or not they like what they see is unimportant. You can be the most unattractive person in the world, but when it comes down to it, money talks.

If you're paranoid about going to a cosmetic counter, at least put your best face forward. At the bare minimum, be well groomed and have some idea of why you're there. If you don't want to spend a lot of dough, tell these bitches exactly what you're looking for. If they try to derail you, stay on point and tell them you'll take samples, if any are available. If you do your research first on what you need for your age and condition, you can get out fairly painlessly. What I mean by age and condition is, for instance, that you'll want anti-wrinkle moisturizer if your skin is younger and one that minimizes if your skin is older.

In my many, many experiences with Cosmetic Counter Bitches, I've found that they lay off a little when you tell them exactly what you have in mind instead of blurting, "Gee, I dunno—what's new?" A question like that just opens the floodgates for any product the company ever made. I suggest that you get to know the bitch behind the counter if you intend to use this company for a while. The best way to do this is to wait until you need a complete system or until you plan to buy at least three decently priced products. I find that if you go headstrong into a company, you'll always come up with at least four items you'll dub "impossible to live without." When you spend a substantial amount of green, it's certain these bitches will love you. They'll tell you about all the upcoming colors, give you samples galore, and possibly sneak in an extra treat here and there. Solid relationships with Cosmetic Counter Bitches are rewarding because you will always be given the star treatment.

I suggest buying from mostly one company, but that's up to you. If you go to different brands (a lip gloss here, a mascara there), you might have trouble getting attention and probably won't get star treatment. Honestly, most of the companies produce quality makeup, so the choice is yours based on what appeals.

The other way to win them over is through good old-fashioned loyalty. You may be fearful that the bitches will forget you after hefty purchases, but have no worries; they won't. You'll be etched in their brains for quite some time. When you don't have the loot to buy a lot, simply buy the same key pieces repeatedly. Sooner rather than later, as you approach the counter, the lip gloss you have claimed for life will be on its way to the checkout.

I had an instance where one store was completely depleted of my beloved eyeliner. One quick call to the boutique in New York was all it took for my eyelid and that eyeliner to be united. It turned out the eyeliner had been discontinued, but somehow I managed to score one of the last ones. Less than a year later, it was back by popular demand. To this day, I'm still going strong with it. I was given that liner on the principle of loyalty. I *deserved* that eyeliner. After all, I've been nothing but a devoted customer for years; it's a piece of my arsenal! When you're loyal like I am, these companies will make it happen for you. I have bounced from city to city, but every time I move, I wait until I need my lip liner, gloss, and lip pencil before bonding with the new Chanel artiste. I get a surge of energy knowing I'm about to turn the bitch's day around.

I flash a grin, I wave, and then I flash my credit card. I draw on my lips, smear them with gloss, and I'm soon sashaying out of the store. I strut away with a perfectly lined glossy sex kitten pout. In an effort to show the world my artwork, I try to remain tight-lipped. Despite these efforts, I can't help but smile. Not only have I walked away with the clutch components of my physical existence; I've walked away with a new friend.

The Cosmetic Counter Bitch is extremely transcendable—which is enough to put a grin on anyone's face. Why not let it put one on yours? After all, you can guarantee your grin will be glossed!

Dump Their Shit On You

Just like toilets, most everyone has a cell phone. *And* Facebook. *And* Twitter. Ugh. Before I go on a rant and puke in the nearest trash can over social media, I should just as soon call a friend. I hate throwing up. The nausea reminds me of the most recent guy I dated—lots of nausea there.

Since puking is not the perfect option, what to do? What the Dump Their Shit on You Bitches do is phone someone and expel their pink-puke nastiness. And in a messed-up way, they like it because they feel better afterwards.

Let us be clever here. Imagine you have a lot to "talk" about … It matters to you a great deal. And the person you want to vent to is available. You can discuss your tax crap, the Chihuahua that shits everywhere, or the fact that you can't secure a Britney Spears front-row seat in Vegas. You *dump* on this person and it sucks terribly, but it feels good too because you've released some (if not all of) your angst.

This is the only time in the book that I will admit I can be guilty of showing some of these characteristics. I have a good friend named Terry that I call all the time. He probably is the one person who listens consistently. Sure, I have other friends that listen too. But Terry has been doing it for years and years and never has *not* listened to me—even if four or five times a day. And these are long conversations, not just "hear about the fabulous Wienerschnitzel I had last night."

What constitutes a Dump Your Shit Bitch is someone who calls you and literally controls the entire conversation and barely lets you get a word in. It's a huge rant from hell, some people's worst nightmare. But, if you're a good friend and care about the bitch, you will listen and do so patiently. I'm still a bitch, though, and I feel bad doing it, but I need someone to listen, so therefore I dump.

The danger is that these bitches take up a very valuable thing, and that's time. We all know time is precious, but so are family and (true) friends. You will know you're definitely dealing with a Dump Their Shit Bitch when you recognize the following criteria: Exceptionally long-winded conversations and the person is angry, upset, hyperactive, or had too many glasses of Cabernet. Exceptionally long-winded conversations because the person keeps repeating himself or herself and usually doesn't realize it. You find yourself short on time afterward and suddenly don't feel like completing your errands, such as going to the gym or the grocery store, because you're so drained.

How to deal? First, acknowledge yourself! Give yourself a good ole pat on the back for being such a fabulous sounding board. Often these conversations can bring out a laugh or two, but often they are really just draining and, as I mentioned, time consuming. Second, ask yourself how often the bitch in question is a repeat offender. Many, many times bitches of all sorts are repeat offenders, but these types require more tough love than slamming down the gavel in the courtroom. Therefore, it's best to simply cut them off when they start to prattle, for you'll already know from their histories where this conversation is going (and that seem like eternity).

If you don't take action by politely cutting them off, you'll find yourself rushing out the door before you miss a cardio class or driving into gridlock because you missed good traffic flow time. And everyone who has been stuck in bad traffic (only to be late or miss an appointment altogether) knows that it's frustrating. And time consuming. And dangerous. After the bitch is done using you as a trash can, you'll be shaking your steering wheel and yelling "Bitch!" at the top of your lungs. Don't feel bad! Dump Your Shit Bitches will call someone else—or two, or three—only God knows—until they finally have released.

Another attractive way of handling these bitches is to explaining that you're out the door or in the middle of something and offer to set up a time to call them back. Or even better, why not get together when you both have time and then you can hear them go on and on? Heck, you may even get a chance to dump it all out too. But that's speculation. Before these bitches waste your time and keep bitching on the phone to you, just stop it in its tracks and *poof*! "Good-bye!"

Scopers

Scopers are people who are feeling out others. They're checking the scene and are in a highly observational mode regarding other people. Scoping can occur across several different levels. A little scope here, a little scope there. A little scoping never hurt anyone because it usually occurs when one is gathering first impressions. However, some people abuse the scope to where they are no longer Scopers and start judging and become nosy. The practice of scoping is somewhat complex because it's not necessarily good, but it's not necessarily bad either. I'm sure we've all heard or have expressed the term in such cases as these:

"Let's scope out the situation."
"Give me the general scope."
"That new club? Let's scope it out on Friday."

Scoping is essential and warranted because not only does it allow you a general overview, but it can also answer any questions you may consider pertinent when getting to know someone. What's more, it can assist you when deciding whether you want to move forward with someone (whether it be for professional, friendship, or romantic reasons). It's getting the gist of that person, if you will.

For these reasons, it's imperative to understand that scoping is common and is bound to happen at times. Because it's so common, there are different levels on which scoping can occur, starting with the physical. Your physical condition—your clothing, hair, skin, and stature—are all up for evaluation. Scopers may or may not like what they see. If they're of the Player Hater nature, then the scope becomes negative. However, a Scoper may adore you, and as a result, the communication process will flow freely.

Scoping can be confusing to people because it's more of bitch trait than a bitch type. It's an act of bitchiness performed by Li'l Bitches—it's not an enthusiastic, genuine "I want to get to know you" vibe. It's looking at you up and down, studying you out of the corners of their eyes, and looking over their shoulders at you. It's a form of scanning—not because the Scopers are truly interested in you but more about what you have, and thus they make personality assumptions from that.

If someone is scoping your house, car, or financial status, then it becomes the *scoping of the assets.* Upon entering your home, one might scope out what type of furniture you have as well as any audio/video equipment. Some may scope more things than others do, depending on what they consider important in a home, as well scope for personality clues, such as what books you've read or what DVDs you've watched. Since scoping mirrors nosiness, it's not uncommon to have a bathroom Scoper—one who looks behind bathroom curtains, under sinks, and inside medicine cabinets.

When it comes to your vehicle, the Scoper will take note of the make, model, and year, and could very well ask you how much your car payments are, if any. A vehicle Scoper may also pay attention to details: Do you have the latest technology installed for music and sound? In addition, he or she may also take note of the car seat material and any other accessories.

When people *scope the scene*, it usually pertains to their being in a public establishment. Restaurants, shopping malls, and movie theatres are all breeding grounds for Scopers. Night clubs are even more likely to produce Scopers since everyone's checking out everyone else. Also, should you throw a party or host a barbecue, you're guaranteed to have a Scoper or two. Scopers carry a high risk of becoming jealous, which, at that point, will bring any bitch tendencies they have out of hiding.

While the scoping in public takes place, the Scoper considers a series of things: Who are you with and what does the person look like? Is your hair, makeup, and clothing appropriate? Do you have to wait in line or are you on the guest list? All this information is absorbed, allowing the Scoper to make subconscious or conscious decisions about who you are.

In reality, scoping, is a way of gathering information. You might not know when you're being scoped, but if you catch anyone staring, especially while out in public, the person is probably sizing you up or feeling you out—in other words, scoping you. Most of the time, there is some envy going on, which is why the Scoper is looking so hard at you. Or if you happen to have this person at your house and you catch him or her closely studying your decor, it's a red flag that there's some envy there.

If you know someone's scoping you out, don't be alarmed. If you realize someone's trying to get the general scope of you, you'll find that often he or she isn't being bitchy, just curious. Recognize and accept that it's happening, and while it is, remember that you can easily scope back too! If the scoping yields a positive result, then congratulations! You've survived this unavoidable act of nonverbal communication. If the result is negative, further scoping may be needed before it becomes positive. If, however, it never becomes positive, then the Scoper may not really be a Scoper but rather one of the bitches we cover herein.

Pushy

With these broads, I feel like I'm getting steamrolled. Or if I were standing on the edge of a cliff, all it would take would be a light poke from her pointy nail and off the deep end I go. Best advice? They push you and you shove back. An all-out tug-of-war for control and standing your ground is what this entails. I don't like to get pushed around, and these bitches push their agendas on you. And it's not cute.

Agendas, agendas, agendas. To conform, to not conform. When it comes to Pushy Bitches, think of yourself as a tree. You have to be grounded and strong so that when the hurricane is coming, you don't get uprooted and blown over. Be strong! Stand your ground!

From peddling door-to-door cosmetics to insurance policies, Pushy Bitches want to close a deal. They can be hard to defuse because they have one hell of a wall around them—hard to knock down—and don't take no for an answer (that is, until your Inner Bitch lashes out and tells them to go sit in the corner). Part of it is not taking no for an answer but also moving things along in their favor. These are frustrating bitches because even when you turn around and tell them no, they're still scooting you along. Steamrolling. Running you over. Damn.

The key is to remember that they're pushing something—even if it's as miniscule as what to order for an appetizer. This isn't a one-time instance, however. This is a *trait* that these bitches possess, and the more you allow them to push, the more they will continue with their behavior.

What's sick about them is that they are essentially testing your limits. How far can they push? If they pushed that far already, why not try for a little more? And the push goes forward and often downward (deeper), into an emotional state of turmoil that's more than just physical. Gosh, talking about it makes me rethink their place in the hierarchy!

How to handle? As I said, you don't push back. You shove. Tell the bitch, "Screw your appetizer," because we know an appetizer is *not* what it's about. It's not about whether or not to have a Wienerschnitzel, and it's not about who will doggy-sit the Chihuahua that shits everywhere. What it *is* about is control, and, even though I'm a huge fan of patience, this bitch gets me running out of time (and we know by now that we have no time to waste). Be flat out and tell the person that he or she is gross. That'll stop the behavior because the word "gross" is gross in itself. Just because somebody isn't physically pushing you doesn't mean that the person isn't still pushing—and if you think about it mentally mental force can be even more damaging than physical force. We were born with the fight-or-flight reaction, and sometimes we can't just fly away.

My grandma Jean used to rest her lovely hands on the sink basin while she washed dishes. She would look out the window and sigh, "I sometimes wish I could sprout wings and fly away." While that comment escaped my attention at the time, I'm now rethinking what exactly she meant. She didn't fly away—she wouldn't have done that out of loyalty to her family—but she didn't fight either. All that bottled-up emotion wreaked havoc on her beautiful body and soul, and she was taken way too soon. She flew away in the form of an angel, but it really wasn't necessary. Upon reflection, I think she felt pushed in some way.

If I had it my way, I would have been more mature during those days and asked what was really going on. People just don't make comments about flying away for no reason. I must have been ten or eleven at the time—not even a step up the "Ladder of Bitch"—but my granny was, and still is, one of the most important people in my life. Thus I draw on her life experience. I would chew and swallow an entire Coast soap bar if that's what it took to bring her back—in fact, I'd do pretty much anything. And I would do it because I'd like to know why she said such things—and moreover, who or what was pushing her around so I could correct it. All in one breath, I would encourage her to get that Inner Bitch stronger and shove back.

Look, I have a strong Inner Bitch, and nothing brings it out more than defense of my loved ones. Remember the mantra? Be 49 percent sweetheart and 51 percent bitch. Don't push it. And with a Pushy Bitch, she's pushing her luck. Again, stand your ground! Be a strong, sturdy tree because in this world, because in this world, someone *will* want to knock you down. Be firm in your beliefs, your values, your heart, and your soul! And believe in yourself as much as you want to breathe. Storms will come, but storms will go, and if you can maintain integrity in your roots, you will glisten in the sunshine with your leaves. That being said, screw Pushy Bitches, bitches!

She Has the Man I Want

I love being in love. The rush of excitement and the thrilling thought of "The One" makes my hair stand on end. Everyone's always on the lookout for Mr. or Ms. Right (unless that person has already been found), even if that person doesn't admit it. Even the stingiest of people want to be in love and be loved. Well, what the heck do you do when you find out *your* one belongs to someone else?

I know, I know—we can't control with whom we fall in love. Whether it's love at first sight or a gradual thing, everyone at some point is going to fall madly head over heels in love. Given that there are billions of people on planet Earth, the chances of having a significant other are fairly high.

People can turn into bitches if they think others are after their sweethearts. This chapter is meant to shed light on your part in the scenario. Even if the couple is married, some would tell you to move in on full throttle. But karma, my friends, acts almost like a boomerang in the universe. With karma, the boomerang brings back *three* times what you send out, whether positive or negative. If you set out to break a happy couple apart, it could backfire in several different ways.

For example, you can't always guarantee that the one you want is into you enough to leave the other person. If you press your luck, he or she might shut you down with a snap. And if such a person screws around with you, what does that say about character? Also, let's say you did end up together. How would you feel if someone tried to steal him or her from you (and succeeded)? Karma! I know it's tough, but the best thing to do is be patient.

I'm sure some of you out there reading this might be ready to throw the book across the room while you screech, "What does this dumb bitch mean *be patient*? And watch my life without this person pass me by? I'll have cobwebs growing off me by the time they break up!" There, there, my lovelies. You *have* to be patient, but you don't have to be nonexistent in the person's world either. This concept is crucial because it's the one thing the significant other can't argue with. We all share this world, and the chances of you and your crush conversing because you work together or go to the same gym, church, cooking class, or Starbucks are good to happen.

You don't have to ignore this person or feel guilty or nervous. This person has obviously affected you in some way to make you have the feelings you have. It doesn't really matter what it was about the person that impacted you. I think most would agree that when we fall in love with someone because of his or her personality, in time this person becomes more appealing physically. If we fall in love because he or she is hot as shit, we're sometimes willing to give the personality a chance (and sometimes fall in love because of looks alone.) Don't feel bad about feelings you can't control. If the craving for this person won't cease, stay in his or her life and try to make contact every so often. But I warn you: move slowly. Since you're walking a fine line, ease up if your ga-ga meter is off the heezy (off the hook).

Remember, we don't want to be bitches. Being around your love interest and gabbing on and on flamboyantly is a turnoff and a bad way to get attention. If you let yourself get in over your head, you might drive yourself crazy. Every time you and the crush exchange words, you'll break apart everything that was said, analyzing it before you stash it away. As the pursuit continues, you'll start stashing more and more and more—until your head explodes.

If you start creating a fantasy world where the two of you exist together, you could be in danger of going there too often. Subconsciously, you'll start to rely on the crush for a fix or else you become saddened. If you find yourself feeling down because the crush doesn't call or you don't speak as much as you like, remember that he or she *is* technically off limits. As I said, if you play too much into the fantasy, you risk forgetting the attachment issue and risk feeling hurt. Even though it's hard to control feelings of desire, you have to be aware of how far you mentally take it. If we could, we'd draw straws when it comes to finding love and turn it off and on at the touch of a button. Yeah, in a perfect world.

Although the person may very well like you, don't panic if the breakup doesn't occur rapidly. He or she may be waiting for more problems to surface so there is a valid reason to break up rather than because of, ahem, you. Furthermore, you haven't the slightest idea what the couple has been through together. Maybe they've been together six months or sixteen years, but for all you know, issues like rehab, pregnancies, or family trauma could have taken place. Such issues could have strengthened the relationship to serious proportions. The two may have shared near-death experiences, such as being struck by lightning together.

I met a couple who was on the verge of calling it quits, so they decided to take a walk outside to talk about it. While they were out, there was a lightning storm, and as they walked hand in hand, a bolt of lightning struck them. People don't just walk around getting struck by lightning together, so they soon took vows to be together forever. We don't know what kinds of situations the couple has experienced, so it's important to be patient and realize that a breakup could take a while.

Even if they haven't shared any serious moments, it can still be difficult for them to let go of one another. We have trouble swearing off cheeseburgers and ice cream, so why would someone we see almost every day be different? It's a habit, and they can be hard to break, mostly because feelings of fear of the unknown are exposed.

Give it time, as it very well could happen. By the same token, you can't wait around forever. While you're waiting, keep your options open. Even though guys in the past had me bent like Beckham, I went on other dates anyway just to keep my sanity. I never threw them in my current love interest's face, however, and neither should you. Here's why.

Your crush will assume you're sleeping with your dates. If you change dates more than your underwear and think you'll look desirable by telling the person, think again. You run the risk of looking promiscuous, so keep your dates on the hush. At the same time, don't let the crush know if you're date*less*. Granted, he or she won't think you're a freak or weird, but it's really nobody else's business. If you talk about anything, talk about interests and hobbies. If this person is meant to be yours, it will happen in due time.

Another reason not to mention anything about seeing anyone is that if this person is interested but even the smallest bit fearful that you've found someone else, then he or she may use it as grounds to not pursue you further. Once again, patience brings rewards. If you're in love with someone and he or she has someone else, you have to be kind. If not for human decency, then do it for the one you love—be sweet as candy! Your crush's bitch may be a nice person, but more than that, the person has more power than you do. Your crush's lover has more control because he or she spends more time with this person. He or she can see the other person longer and have hours in a day to rekindle any suffering flame.

If you've caught your crush's interest and the other lover catches on, you could be in for quite a loop. This person could fight over his or her love, and no one could be blamed! Hence, it's critical that you be cordial and pleasant. Anything less gives the person live ammo and could possibly alter your crush's view of you into something negative. If you're unpleasant to the person's lover, he or she could retaliate by pointing out your behavior, thus turning off the crush. Don't screw yourself! If you're pleasant and dispense no negativity, then nothing negative can be said about you. If you display nothing but kindness and the lover badgers you anyway, then your crush will see there are no grounds for ridicule and could write your rival off as a Player Hater. The key is to be casual and friendly. Being kind will also help ease the lover's fears—in other words, it can assist him or her in letting the guard down. This is not to say you have to kiss ass, but being pleasant and kind has other benefits:

1) You feel good about yourself and your sincerity in the situation, which will come across when interacting with the person. The behavior shows that you are *not* a player.
2) Your crush will appreciate your making things easier.
3) You'll learn more details about their courtship, including juicy gossip and details about both characters (assuming you're in close contact.)

The key element to making a situation like this work for you is to concentrate on giving a sincere effort in eliminating any hate you have stored within you. While it's normal to be envious at times, it's doesn't mean it's appropriate or warranted. If you're born jealous, then you must pay careful attention to the envy you exert. Envy, jealousy, hate—call it what you want but it boils down to nothing but negative … all the way around!

Crushes can be fun, but remember, your crush is spoken for, at least temporarily! Keep it at a level where you admire from afar. Look but don't touch—you get the point! Don't give all your energy away either. Save your energy for yourself and take in the crush's energy when there's an even exchange. Think Goldilocks—not too much, not too little, just the right amount.

Another thing to think about is that people like to decide for themselves what they want. This autonomy is normal. So be platonic, your own sweet self, and leave the door open. When you open the door, it gives your crush an easy entrance.

I can't reiterate enough the importance of patience. As the saying goes, "The best things come to those who wait." Well this, my friends, is no exception. Ride the waves and don't ask them where they go—just have faith, keep your love boat afloat, and set your sights on the horizon. The sea of love is a vast and wide one; don't get hook, lined, and sunk over a spoken-for fish— if you do this, you could miss out on a whale of a time!

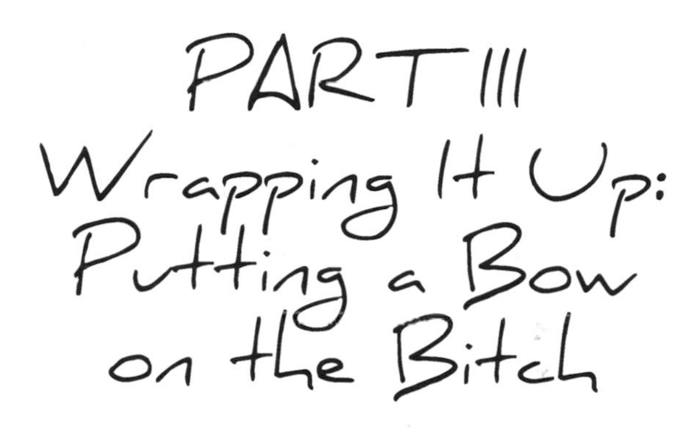
PART III
Wrapping It Up:
Putting a Bow
on the Bitch

When Bitches Come Back

I think you'll agree that for the most part, bitches can be transcended. Some will be transcended completely once you communicate with them and make them understand that you won't tolerate their behavior. If the bitches were Player Haters and finally had breakthroughs (no longer seeing you as a threat), then they could very well be prepared to be the friends they should've been since the beginning. This is rare, but it can happen. It's up to you to make the decision about whether they're sincere, and if they are, be sure they have completely let go of any jealousy.

If there is a reconciliation of some sort, however, be on guard when you introduce this person back into your life. Don't just try to pick up where you left off. Life is precious and so is time, and it's not meant to be spent waiting for someone else to come through for the better. You're better off without the person, even if it means being alone. Ask yourself:

1) Am I accepting this person back because I feel bad saying no?
2) Has he or she really changed?
3) Why now—after so many months or years?
4) How much of the benefit of the doubt am I giving?

If you do get back into contact with these former bitches, take time to evaluate their current attitudes toward life. During conversations, are they battering someone? Do they sound bitter? I would never recommend contacting a Player Hater after having a fallout. As long as these bitches are the way they are, they won't really take the time to appreciate that you're giving them a second chance to redeem themselves.

Classic Bitch Came Back Stories: When I first moved to my current location, I was quickly introduced to my first batch of friends. All of them—in some way, shape, or form—were bitches. What was worse, they were of the player hating nature. I got to know these bitches pretty well, and after giving them six months of time, gas, and energy, what I had to show for it can only be compared to a dagger in the back.

According to the basic rules of survival, one should never remove an object from a deep wound unless done by a professional. You have a higher chance of survival if you leave it, because should it be removed, one could bleed to death. I carried that dagger, which was one of a few, in my back for damn near a year. I got used to it.

I had a fallout with two girls, and as the one-year mark of the fallout approached, one of these bitches threw herself a birthday party. The mutual friend that introduced us begged me to go because she dreaded going to the party solo. I hadn't spoken to or seen these bitches in months. One was a major Player Hater, the other her Scrappy-Doo.

At first I thought, *What the heck. It's a party.* Then my mail arrived. Sent to me was my brain, which I quickly placed back into my head. I called the mutual friend and expressed my desire not to go. I didn't think it was such a good idea. I couldn't have cared less what those two girls thought, and while they seemed to think the idea was dandy, my Inner Bitch told me otherwise.

Had I considered going because there were no other parties that evening? Hardly. Was I going to reconcile? Not a chance. The fact of the matter was that I had gone so long in solitude without them that to reintroduce negativity to my life was unthinkable. Let's shoot ahead in this story about two months. It's a gorgeous day, and I'm charging along in my truck on I-10. The sun is out, and the weather is perfect. Life is sweet. My cell rings, and I flip it open. I don't recognize the number, but it's my area code. Reluctantly I answer. It's the Player Hater herself! I can't believe my ears. As usual, I play it cool. She, as usual, sounds quite phony.

"So how are things for you?" she coos.
"Oh, things are just great! Same ol', same ol'." (No wonder it's called small talk!)

She says she's been thinking of me because we spent the last Fourth of July together, which resulted in her getting involved in a fistfight at a party—I didn't participate. I tell her I already have plans for the Fourth (which I do, and they're undoubtedly better than her plans). We close with the typical exchange:

"Well, thanks for calling. Bye."
"Call me sometime," she says.
"Oh, yeah, sure, if I'm in your area," I reply.

I snap my phone shut and shake my head. Did that conversation just take place? Indeed.

That day, I felt my karma had come full circle. There was a strange but small satisfaction in her calling me. What prompted her to call? I haven't the faintest idea. She probably smoked an obscene amount of marijuana, scrolled through her phone, and hastily pressed dial. The sweat beaded up on her forehead as she waited—one, two, three rings. The fact that the hater called *last* put me in the position of having the final word, which was not to call her back. That small power probably meant more to her than it did to me. Nevertheless, it was still a nice gesture on karma's side. It served as a reminder that I am a sweetheart and she's a hater.

I encourage you to ask the questions I posed earlier. What will you really gain out of accepting someone back into your world? Can you do better? I'd take his or her "reach out" and wave it around proudly. You've earned it. But don't be a fool—if you do become friends with this person and he or she dupes you, you've just wasted more time and energy on something you probably already knew. Give yourself some credit. You're better than that!

Voices will come back—not necessarily to haunt but rather to give you closure. The Male Bitch that served as the basis for that chapter miraculously resurfaced just two days after the Player Hater Bitch!

In the past, I had only spoken only words of love, praise, and all things positive about him. I had dreamt of and created the perfect portrait of this guy. What I expected him to be was much more elaborate and much more extravagant than the real deal. I don't doubt this guy could've become what I had conjured, but it certainly didn't pan out that way. I think that I put him on such a pedestal that I forgot how lucky *he* was to attract me.

After four years of intense wonder, yearning, and restrained passion, the Male Bitch and I finally hooked up. It wasn't the Olympics of lovemaking, but it was important to me in that, for the first time in my sexual history, it was *completely* okay for someone to take me. The first time we kissed, I felt the earth move under my feet. I was totally mesmerized and, worse yet, hopelessly in love with this fool.

It was so awful that my desire suppressed my energy when I was with him. I was so nervous that I could barely speak! One look at him and I was completely shut down. He went bitch when he laid me instead of first laying his cards down and saying, "Look, I like you, but I'm seeing someone." I found out later that he was, and although not a full-fledged girlfriend, she was enough to be a cock block. Instead, he didn't explain shit. No answering my phone calls and no acknowledging my e-mails, which I *know* I am the bomb at writing! I knew if I couldn't bring him back through e-mails that he was gone for good. He sealed the deal with a grand slam and ran into the dugout never to return, or so I thought at the time.

More than a year had passed since I sent him backpacking out of my life, but through serendipity, he was hiking right back in. Our reunion seemed like a fluke—he was visiting our college town back in Florida and randomly ran into my Top Male Dog (another term for best friend). The two hit it off, and before you knew it, they realized they *both* knew me. My Top Dog made quite an impression. It finally must have clicked because not even a month thereafter, I received the apologetic e-mail. Had he never met my Top Male Dog randomly in the flesh, he may have never been prompted to apologize. If I were then who I am now, I wouldn't give two craps (or one, for that matter), but as I said earlier, closure plays a large role, and it certainly did in this case.

The reason bitches come back can differ from bitch to bitch, which will ultimately have an effect on the final outcome. My best advice is to evaluate each for what it is and realize you have options. You don't have to shun anyone, and you don't have to let anyone back in. Be aware of the past, the actions they took, and examine how you felt when at your lowest point with that person. Consider the questions posed earlier and try your best to see where this person fits in your life. If you let certain people be part of your life again, what roles will they play in it? Do you think they'd be a positive or a negative?

It pays to take the time to evaluate your relationships with people and what you expect to learn and gain from them. Unfortunately, engaging in hard thinking as such can bring about emotions we don't want to face. We're forced to truly examine people, and the results can be uneasy. When it comes to bitches you've dealt with in the past, use simple caution. If they say they're truly sorry and you believe them, then it's certainly gracious of you to forgive.

I love you, bitch

As I close this book, I want to emphasize that a bitch can motivate or inspire you. The experience may be so terrible that you kill the relationship, but it can also live because you *live and learn.* There are so many ways to defuse a bitch; that's up to you. You must refer to *The Book of Bitches* to really grasp what the heck is going on. What are you going to accept from bitches? What are you *not* going to accept? Only you can answer these questions. But take time to make your decision because you want to be as prepared as possible in this wild kingdom of bitch. Know your morals, know your values, and know your integrity level. You must maintain a certain level of integrity at all times, and your Inner Bitch is there to balance you.

You *must* buck up in this world of bitch. I didn't write this book for my health; I wrote it for yours. I'm giving you this information because the universe assigned it to me. *The Book of Bitches* isn't the Holy Grail, but it's not barbaric (think Genghis Khan) in the advice given herein.

We can't hope that bitches will go away by themselves, because they won't. Even if you have a situation where you feel you haven't been able to transcend and defuse a bitch, think positively: the person is out of your life, and you have the wisdom to see it for what it is. You want results, and The Book of Bitches gives you them! Even if you can't salvage a relationship, be thankful for all bitch experiences in your life quest to be stronger. Just smile and say, "I love you, bitch!" You will deal with bitches constantly, so if you don't understand by now, then you need to do one of the following:

1) Go get yourself some prescription bifocal eyeglasses and read the book again.
2) Go get yourself some colored contacts and let your Inner Bitch read the book again.
3) If push comes to shove, pick up the nearest phone and dial 1-800-eff-U, bitch! Just kidding. Just read again and know that with every read, you will absorb more of the lessons.

Just own it and pay attention to how you feel because people around you only get so many chances. Some don't ever get a shot at the brass ring when it comes to a relationship with you, and they don't deserve one either.

It took me years to compile, organize, and transcribe a lifetime of bitch experiences. It's so rewarding to be able to take these experiences (even though at times they were negative) and produce something positive and entertaining. I hope that you not only appreciate the work but also that you'll apply my ideas to your daily life.

Life is a journey. It's exciting, empowering, and uplifting, but without the right approach and perspective, it can be frightening and debilitating, weighing heavily on one's mind. Also, what you give you'll certainly get in return, so displaying a tough as nails persona will only make life tough for you. Don't be a bitch. Be happy! And if you find yourself grunting along, slamming cabinets, and giving the finger to motorists, then take a good look in the mirror and ask yourself why. Be honest with yourself before you settle in your bitch ways and someone has to rip off your dusty bitch shades so you can see the light.

We owe one another a certain degree of compassion, empathy, and respect. By paying careful attention to the attitudes we exude, we can spare others distress, irritation, and heartbreak. However, committing to a bitchy attitude will cause the road of life to be bumpy, making it difficult for others, including yourself, to journey smoothly. Compassion, empathy, respect—these are elements of fluidity. And if you come across someone who hasn't seen the light, don't kick into overdrive and run your wheels over the bump that person created. You're entitled to a smooth ride, so instead throw it in reverse, take an alternative route, and pave the way for the others. Don't be afraid either! You're armed with your Inner Bitch, and you can handle anything! As I stated previously, life isn't a game or a race—it's a gift. It's something to be treasured and shared, not hoarded and fought over. So please don't be bitches to one another, for our days aren't limitless. Since there's not an Inner Bitch in this world strong enough to save us all, we must each do our part.

Strive for the better good, and above all, be good to each other. Finally, I hope that in your quest for paradise (where the sand is soft and white and the ocean is clear and bright), you remember to lie back, sip a tropical concoction with an umbrella in it, and smile. You've earned it, for you've just graduated from the University of Bitch. Congratulations! Applause, applause, applause!

Erika Lisa Valdez is an expert on bitches. A beauty queen from age four, she's weeded her way through them on a daily basis—at school, on pageant stages and TV sets, and in everyday relationships. She now holds more than thirty-five pageant titles and has become a popular entertainment personality, appearing in national magazines such as *Maxim* and *Stuff* and on television shows such as *The Price is Right* as a Barker Beauty and *Wild On!* as a Panama City correspondent.

Owner of the pageant consulting firm Time for the Tiara, Valdez ensures her clients regularly win coveted titles on a local, state, and national basis. She is a former homecoming queen and senior class president, and is a graduate of Florida State University with a degree in pre-law Communications and political science.

Valdez is also the author of *My Sister Can Fly On a Broomstick* and *It's Our Pleasure: An Insider's Guide to Navigating a Five-Star Hotel.*

Made in the USA
San Bernardino, CA
29 July 2015